CONFLICT AND SOLIDARITY IN A
GUIANESE PLANTATION

T0270851

LONDON SCHOOL OF ECONOMICS
MONOGRAPHS ON SOCIAL ANTHROPOLOGY

Managing Editor: Dr Paul Stirling

The Monographs on Social Anthropology were established in 1940 and aim to publish results of modern anthropological research of primary interest to specialists.

The continuation of the series was made possible by a grant in aid from the Wenner-Gren Foundation for Anthropological Research, and more recently by a further grant from the Governors of the London School of Economics and Political Science. Income from sales is returned to a revolving fund to assist further publications.

The Monographs are under the direction of an Editorial Board associated with the Department of Anthropology of the London School of Economics and Political Science.

The Editorial Committee most gratefully acknowledges a generous subvention from the Booker Group towards the cost of publishing this volume.

LONDON SCHOOL OF ECONOMICS
MONOGRAPHS ON SOCIAL ANTHROPOLOGY
No. 25

Conflict and Solidarity in a Guianese Plantation

by

CHANDRA JAYAWARDENA

Routledge
Taylor & Francis Group

LONDON AND NEW YORK

First published 1963 by THE ATHLONE PRESS

Published 2020 by Routledge
2 Park Square, Milton Park, Abingdon, Oxon OX14 4RN
605 Third Avenue, New York, NY 10017

First issued in paperback 2021

Routledge is an imprint of the Taylor & Francis Group, an informa business

© *Chandra Jayawardena,* 1963

Notice:
Product or corporate names may be trademarks or registered trademarks, and are
used only for identification and explanation without intent to infringe.

Publisher's Note
The publisher has gone to great lengths to ensure the quality of this reprint but
points out that some imperfections in the original copies may be apparent.

ISBN 13: 978-0-367-71685-1 (pbk)
ISBN 13: 978-1-84520-020-6 (hbk)

TO THE PEOPLE OF
ROSIGNOL, BLAIRMONT AND
PORT MOURANT

There is, in fact, a manly and lawful passion for equality which incites men to wish all to be powerful and honoured.

Alexis De Tocqueville
Democracy in America

Preface

THIS study[1] concerns two communities of sugar plantation labourers, the descendants of indentured immigrants from India, who live in the county of Berbice, British Guiana. The study is focused on the analysis of social conflict: the factors that cause it, the forms it takes and its social consequences. I have sacrificed comprehensiveness for detail, in order to present an intensive analysis of a particular type of conflict which is expressed in interpersonal disputes over prestige, and which occurs with striking frequency in Guianese plantations.

These disputes are analysed in relation to the social system in which they occur. In recent years there has been an increasing interest among social anthropologists and sociologists in the analysis of social conflict. Emphasis has veered from the anomic character of conflict to its possible integrative functions. The aim of this study is to place expressions of a certain type of conflict in their social setting and, by doing so, to explore the validity of propositions concerning the positive functions of conflict.

In Chapters 1–3 I outline the social system of the plantation, indicating only the basic norms and values governing community life. In Chapters 4 and 5 I discuss the social processes leading to breach of these norms, and analyse concrete instances of the resultant disputes. In Chapters 6 and 7 I consider the extent to which these disputes are controlled by informal sanctions and by courts of law. Chapter 8 is devoted to an interpretation of the consequences of these disputes for the social system of the plantation.

My research in the two plantations was part of a larger project of the Institute of Social and Economic Research, University College of the West Indies, for the study of the East Indians of British Guiana. Dr R. T. Smith, who was in charge of the project, studied East Indians in the rice-growing areas of West Coast Demerara and social groupings among Indian urban residents in Georgetown.

I carried out fieldwork in Blairmont, a plantation in West Coast Berbice, between August 1956 and September 1957, and in Port Mourant, a plantation in Corentyne, Berbice, between February and July 1958. In addition to observation and informal interviews, I conducted a survey to obtain quantitative data on such topics as household composition, marriage, caste, occupation, religious affiliation, income, and experience of the law-courts. I was aided in this task by Mr Nowrang H. Prasad and Mr Bisnath

---

[1] This monograph is a part of a Ph.D. thesis presented at London University in 1959. I have condensed the data on social structure in order to present fully the material on social conflict.

Ramdewar; I take this opportunity to thank them for their great assistance. In collecting information on disputes, I supplemented observation and first- and second-hand reports by consulting police files on adjudicated cases, the records of disputes arbitrated by plantation managers, and the records of the Magistrates' Courts of Berbice.

I cannot say exactly how far the generalizations I have drawn apply to other plantation communities in British Guiana. I have preferred to concentrate on Blairmont because it is the smaller of the two plantations and therefore easier to grasp in its entirety, and also because I spent a much longer time there. However, the social systems of the two plantations are essentially similar, though that of Port Mourant is somewhat more complex. The disputes which are the main subject of this study occur with similar frequency and in similar circumstances in both plantations. I have discussed specific disputes which occurred in one plantation with residents of another; their comments, explanations and attitudes were strikingly similar.

I visited the other plantations of Berbice quite often and feel satisfied that the disputes and concomitant factors discussed here prevail in those plantations too. I believe that what happens in the Berbice plantations also happens to a greater or lesser degree in the plantations of Demerara, because it is unlikely that conditions in Demerara differ radically from those in Berbice. No inquiries into this matter revealed any significant differences. My references to 'the Guianese plantation' should be accepted with these reservations.

It has been impossible to avoid the use of actual place-names, but the names of all persons are fictitious though typical. In order to protect further the anonymity of the persons referred to, I have, as far as possible, refrained from indicating in which of the two plantations the disputes described here occurred. Ten of them occurred in Blairmont and five in Port Mourant.

My research was made possible by the generous financial assistance and co-operation of the Booker Group. While thanking the personnel of this organization, I wish to acknowledge especially the co-operation of the Administrative Manager and Staff of Plantation Blairmont. I am grateful for the valuable assistance I received from Mr J. E. Adams and Mr L. Narain, then Labour Inspectors of Berbice, Mr Thomas Budhoo of the Rice Producers' Association, the British Guiana Police Force, particularly the constables of the Blairmont Police Station, and the magistrates and lawyers of Berbice, especially Mr Eric Clarke and Mr Louis A. Low. Dr Cheddi Jagan and Mrs Janet Jagan showed much interest in my research and helped me in many ways.

In writing this book I have benefited greatly from the advice and criticism of my teachers in the Department of Anthropology, London School of Economics, my colleagues at the Institute of Social and Economic Research, University College of the West Indies, and my present associates in the Department of Anthropology, University of Sydney. I wish to acknowledge special debts of gratitude to Dr Maurice Freedman who, as my supervisor, advised and encouraged me through all stages of this work, and to Dr R. T. Smith who introduced me to fieldwork with great patience and understanding and gave me all the advice and help I required. I am grateful to Professor Max Gluckman for his valuable and constructive criticisms. I thank my wife for helping me to prepare this manuscript for publication, and Mrs B. Hooke for her editorial assistance.

The people of British Guiana are well known in the West Indies for their hospitality and my own experience certainly confirms this reputation. Unable to repay all the kindness and favours they showered on me, I dedicate this book to my friends in Rosignol, Blairmont and Port Mourant as an expression of my friendship and gratitude.

C. J.

Department of Anthropology
University of Sydney
October 1961

Contents

Tables

I

Introduction

BRITISH Guiana is situated in the north-eastern corner of South America. It is bounded on the north by the Caribbean Sea, on the west by Venezuela, on the south by Brazil, and on the east by Surinam (Dutch Guiana). Although its geographical position suggests that it is a 'Latin American' country, every other consideration underlines its affiliations with the West Indies, and this view is implicit throughout this study.

British Guiana has an area of 83,000 sq. miles. It is traversed from south to north by four rivers: the Essequibo, Demerara, Berbice and Corentyne. The country is divided into three counties named after these rivers — Essequibo, Demerara, and Berbice. The portion of Berbice which lies between the Berbice and Corentyne rivers is known as Corentyne. The Corentyne river forms the boundary between British Guiana and Surinam.

The population, estimated at the end of 1956 to be 506,900,[1] is concentrated within a narrow coastal strip, seldom more than eight miles wide; about 88 per cent of the people live on about 2·5 per cent of the total land area, and nearly four-fifths of the population inhabit the rural settlements which cluster along either side of the public road that stretches through the coastal belt. High tides from the north and river floods from the south are a constant menace to this coastal area, and human life and agriculture have been made possible only by maintaining a costly sea-defence and drainage system.

The main crops are rice and sugar cane. Rice is cultivated over an area of 137,000 acres and is mainly a peasant crop; the average size of a rice farm is from 3 to 10 acres.[2] Sugar cane, which occupies a total area of 81,108 acres,[3] is almost exclusively grown on large, company-owned plantations, of an average size of 8,000–9,000 acres.[4]

Employment in the sugar industry is seasonal, but the number of persons employed—estimated at about 27,000 each week[5]—is greater than in any other form of economic activity. More than half this labour force lives on the plantations. In 1946, out of a total population of 375,701, 75,792, or roughly 20 per cent, were plantation residents, and the proportion at the present time cannot be much less.

[1] *Annual Report of the Registrar General*, 1956.
[2] Smith, 1957.   [3] *Report of the Registrar General*, 1956.
[4] *Report*, 1949, p. 18.   [5] ibid., p. 51.

Though the cattle and timber industries are gradually finding markets abroad, the only important export, apart from rice and sugar, is bauxite which is rapidly becoming a major source of wealth. Sugar production, however, plays a dominant role in the economy of the colony, and the plantation occupies a significant place in the culture of Guianese society.

Among the first Europeans to visit British Guiana were Sir Walter Raleigh and his crew who, in the sixteenth century, sailed up the Essequibo River in quest of the fabulous city of El Dorado. Subsequent Dutch, French and British settlers confined their activities at first to maintaining trading posts. Gradually they opened up cotton, coffee, and sugar plantations and colonized the riverine and coastal regions. As commercial activities and political struggles increased, the indigenous Amerindian tribes retreated further and further into the forests. The labour requirements of the plantations were met by importing labourers, at various periods, from West Africa, Madeira, the West Indian islands, China and India. The present population is composed chiefly of the descendants of these immigrants who came to the country either voluntarily or as indentured labourers or slaves and settled in and around the plantations.

By and large the history of British Guiana can be seen as a process of integrating these diverse immigrant groups to form a single society, facilitated by the increasing power of the State to regulate social relationships. This increase of power was gained at the expense of the local 'plantocracy'. It was achieved here, as in other parts of the West Indies, by a prolonged debate in the nineteenth and early twentieth centuries between colonial governors and the local planter pressure groups, with the Secretary of State for the Colonies as the arbitrator.

The importation of labourers from various parts of the world has resulted in an ethnically heterogeneous population. The population estimates for 1956 provide the following figures[1]:

TABLE I

Population of British Guiana, 1956

	Males	Females	Total
East Indian	122,620	116,330	238,950
African descent	84,950	90,210	175,160
Mixed	27,830	29,420	57,250
Chinese	1,770	1,570	3,340
Portuguese	3,580	4,240	7,820
Other European	1,980	2,400	4,380
Amerindians	10,220	9,780	20,000
	252,950	253,950	506,900

The interweaving strands of several diverse cultures have greatly enriched

[1] *Report*, 1956.

the content of 'creole culture'.[1] In addition to the immigrant labourers, there were generations of Dutch, French, Scottish and English rulers and planters who, by virtue of their dominant positions, left a strong impress on the local culture. One expression of this is the diverse origin of place-names: Vryheid's Lust, La Bonne Intention, Blairmont, Bath, Rampoor and Rupununi. A consideration more germane to this study is the existence of a variety of groups distinguished from each other by differing cultural practices, each seeking, to varying degrees and in varying contexts, to maintain its identity.

In ethnic structure the resident populations of plantations are not representative of the wider society. After Emancipation (1834), the freed Negro slaves left the plantations and settled in the villages, where small-scale farming freed them from the necessity of working for the plantations. Although many Negroes still do so, very few of them are plantation residents. The Portuguese (from Madeira) and the Chinese did not remain on the plantations for long, and hardly any are found on them today. Most members of these two ethnic groups run small- to medium-sized businesses or work as shop-assistants, clerks and executives in big business firms, or have positions in the professions and the civil service. At present, the resident populations of the plantations consist largely of the descendants of the most recent immigrants—the East Indians.[2] The small groups of resident management personnel are 'Other European', reinforced occasionally by a Portuguese or a Mixed person of light complexion.

THE TWO PLANTATIONS

The sugar plantations are laid out on very much the same pattern. The factory, if there is one,[3] borders the main highway of the plantation; near the factory is the 'office', which is the administrative centre; and the hospital. The factory, the office, and the hospital, surrounded by the bungalows of the managerial staff, may be described as the centre of the plantation, from which radiate, usually up to a distance of one or two miles, clusters of labourers' dwellings, and beyond these are the cane-fields.

[1] 'Creole' is a French word which has been adopted into the West Indian vocabulary. It is derived from the Spanish 'criollo', meaning 'native to the locality'. It was originally used by the South American Negroes and Spaniards to distinguish their own children from Negroes and Spaniards freshly arrived from Africa and Spain. This meaning has now been extended to refer to any item of local origin, distinguishing it, on the one hand, from what was recently imported from Europe, Africa, China or India, and, on the other, from what is aboriginal. The word is used in such expressions as 'creole-born', 'creole-music', 'creole-food', 'creole-cattle', etc. For an interesting discussion of 'creole culture' see Adams, 1959.

[2] The descendants of immigrants from India are known in British Guiana as 'East Indians', in order to distinguish them from the aboriginal 'Amerindians'. Unless the context requires the prefix 'East', they will be referred to in the rest of this study as 'Indians'.

[3] Not all plantations have their own factories; those which do not send their cane to the nearest factory.

As was mentioned earlier (see p. 1) only a complicated system of drainage and irrigation makes agriculture in the coastlands possible. The plantation is defended against the sea by a sea-dam, and from the water-logged savannahs behind it by what is known as a back-dam. Water for irrigation is obtained through sluices ('kokers') in the back-dam and is distributed through a series of canals, the banks of which are also known as dams; waste water is drained into the sea through sluices in the sea-dam.

Houses in the plantations, as elsewhere in British Guiana, are usually made of wood and roofed with zinc sheets or wooden tiles. The floors rest on hardwood posts because the low-lying coastlands become very muddy and water-logged during the heavy rains, and the houses are approached by stairways leading to a landing outside the front door. Usually there is a back stairway leading to the kitchen.

The spacious bungalows of the managerial staff are surrounded by well-kept lawns which clearly demarcate the area reserved for members of this group and their families. In some plantations this reservation may be emphasized by a sentry-box.

Labourers' houses are of three types. One is the long low barracks, known as 'logies' or 'ranges', in which the indentured labourers were quartered. They are now partitioned into tenements, each housing one family, and consisting of a little gallery in front, a centre bedroom, and a little gallery at the back which serves as a kitchen. Only a few of these remain today for, as the living conditions of labourers improved, rows of cottages were built. These are larger than tenements and consist of a front gallery, a centre living-room, one or two bedrooms, and a kitchen. The third type of house came into being through the 'Extra-Nuclear Housing Scheme'. Under this scheme the management of plantations set apart portions of land from which plots were leased at nominal rents to labourers who wished to build houses there. Most of the inhabitants of the ranges are thus being re-housed in Extra-Nuclear Settlements. The lessee receives a loan of $1,000[1] which will meet about two-thirds of the building costs of an average-sized house. The type of house to be built, the materials used, and the spending of the loan are subject to the control of the Housing Officer, a management official.

The labourers' dwellings on the plantation are situated by the larger canals which may be used for bathing and washing; drinking water is provided by a public 'stand-pipe'. The land immediately adjacent to a house is the private domain of the occupier and is usually demarcated by a fence or drain; the land beneath the house, known as 'bottom house', serves as a living room during the day.

Blairmont

Blairmont, about 68 miles from Georgetown, is situated on the western bank of the Berbice River between the villages of Rosignol and Ithaca. The

[1] One West Indian dollar is equivalent to 4s. 2d. sterling.

labourers' dwellings are strung out along the public road which traverses the northern boundary of the plantation and leads to the company-owned ferry. There are six dwelling-areas, each consisting of one or more rows of houses, known as Plantain Walk, Forty Three, New Range, Factory Square, Old Yard, Riverside Settlement, and Rampoor; the last, about three miles inland, is connected to the public road by the dam of the main irrigation canal. The cane-fields lie beyond the housing areas, extending about eight to fourteen miles to the back-dam which marks the boundary between the plantation and the savannahs.

The company owns all the houses except those in Riverside Settlement, which came into being through the Extra-Nuclear Housing Scheme. There is a privately-owned store on the plantation which caters for most needs of the residents (rice, salt fish, tinned foods, pressure lanterns, religious pictures, tools, etc.), and several less comprehensive shops known as 'cake-shops' which sell bottled drinks, sweets, snacks, and tinned foods.

An open space between the factory and the office serves as a centre of recreational life where, in the evening, people meet to gossip, argue, drink, and play cards and dominoes. Daily markets and union and political meetings are also held here. The pay-office, the Hindu temple, the mosque, the rum-shop, the school and the cricket ground are all situated in the vicinity.

In 1956-7 there were 451 households in Blairmont (excluding those of managerial personnel). The following table shows the ethnic classification of households in each dwelling-area:

TABLE 2

Ethnic Classification of Households, Blairmont 1956-7

	Indian	Negro	Coloured	Total
Plantain Walk	20	7	1	28
Forty Three	62	11	—	73
New Range	19	6	—	25
Factory Square	5	19	—	24
Old Yard	79	2	—	81
Riverside Settlement	126	2	—	128
Rampoor	91	1	—	92
Total	402	48	1	451

89 per cent of the households are Indian, including five households of Indian women married to Negroes; these, although they occupy a marginal position in the local Indian community, tend to identify themselves with it in many contexts, while the Indians include these mixed households in their activities more readily than Negro households.

The population of Blairmont is almost entirely engaged in sugar production. Except for a few who have been given permission to run a business, every adult male is expected to work for the plantation. The management has the right to refuse accommodation to those who earn their living elsewhere. There is less control over the residents of the Settlement, but there other factors inhibit outside employment. Thus the whole population is organized as a labour force.

The working population is graded in an occupational-cum-social status hierarchy, at the top of which is a largely European managerial group. The middle stratum consists of clerks, foremen and drivers (foremen of field labour gangs). Below them are the field labourers, artisans and mechanics. In this study members of the upper managerial group are excluded except in so far as their actions directly concern the labourers. The clerks and, to a smaller extent, the drivers and foremen are not lower stratum, but they have been included because of the nexus of relationships that binds them to the labourers in other contexts.

It is relatively easy to demarcate Blairmont territorially. The territory of the plantation, except for the public road, is company property. Bounded on one side by the river and on the other by the bush, Blairmont is geographically a cul-de-sac. People go there to work or to visit friends and relatives, but for very little else. There is hardly any economic activity except wage labour, and practically no avenues of upward social mobility exist other than the bottleneck at the driver and clerical grade. Most ambitious and prospering persons leave the plantation for the villages and towns. Blairmont is a cul-de-sac in more senses than one.

The residents see themselves as belonging to Blairmont as opposed to Rosignol and Ithaca. All live in houses owned or controlled by the management, which exercises a general control over their activities as well. The neighbouring villages of Rosignol and Ithaca come under the administration of the District Commissioner; Blairmont does not and local-government functions are fulfilled by management. Most important associations of the labourers, especially those with a religious basis, are organized at the plantation level.

Nevertheless, the plantation is not a self-contained unit in the district. There is a regular contact between Blairmont and the neighbouring villages, as well as with the town of New Amsterdam across the Berbice River. Many plantation residents patronize the stores, cake-shops and drug-stores at Rosignol, and the cinema there provides entertainment for the whole of West Coast Berbice. The company launch plies across the river several times a day, taking people to New Amsterdam to shop, huckster or amuse themselves. The Saturday market at Blairmont attracts crowds from the neighbouring villages.

Port Mourant

Port Mourant, on the Corentyne coast, is about fourteen miles from New Amsterdam. The dwelling-areas, named Bound Yard, Free Yard, Ankerville, Miss Phoebe, and the Settlement, are strung out on either side of the public road that runs eastwards from New Amsterdam to Springlands, on the Corentyne River. Bound Yard consists of ranges and corresponds to the Old Yard of Blairmont, and Free Yard to the company-owned cottage areas. Ankerville and Miss Phoebe are settlements in which labourers have built their own houses on plantation land. This occurred about fifty years ago, long before the Extra-Nuclear Housing Scheme was started. One important difference between Blairmont and Port Mourant is the much larger proportion of labourer-owned housing in the latter. Next to Miss Phoebe is the Port Mourant Settlement which corresponds to the Riverside Settlement of Blairmont.

There are 1,244 houses on company-owned land (excluding the houses of managerial personnel). The number of households is probably higher than this because occasionally two households occupy one house. There are about 17 Negro, 2 Chinese, and 31 Mixed families. In the following Table, I have excluded one section of company-owned land, known as Portuguese Quarter, because, although it belongs to the Company, it is in most respects part of the village of Rosehall. Few of its residents work for the plantation; most of the Mixed families live here. The rest of the population is Indian. Houses are distributed as follows:

TABLE 3

Distribution of Houses, Port Mourant 1957

Dwelling-area	No. of Houses
Bound Yard	114
Free Yard	139
Ankerville	338
Miss Phoebe	188
Settlement	368
	1,147

Not more than fifteen households are Negro. The proportion of Indian households can thus be estimated at about 99 per cent.

The total population of Blairmont in 1956 was about 2,564; the total population of Port Mourant in 1957 was about 9,272. These figures are, of course, exclusive of managerial personnel who, in each plantation, consist of about a score of adult males, some of whom are married and have children.

Port Mourant is very similar to Blairmont in most respects. Both are owned by the same company and both have resident labouring populations. Until 1955 Port Mourant had its own factory. In both the same occupational hierarchy may be seen, ranging from managerial personnel to field labourers. The labour force in each plantation is predominantly Indian and is organized along identical lines.

But although the basic pattern is very much the same, Port Mourant differs from Blairmont in some respects. Since the population of the former is much larger, it has many more stores and cake-shops as well as such specialized establishments as tailors', tinkers' and barbers' shops. It has more than one daily market, though the principal one is held on a green opposite the office and the now dismantled factory. Political and union meetings are held here. There are two Hindu temples, two mosques, one church (Canadian Mission), as well as the places of worship of two other religious sects not found in Blairmont.

For several decades Corentyne has been a more prosperous and developed area than West Coast Berbice. There have been many more sugar plantations providing more avenues for employment and capital accumulation; at present there are five in Corentyne as compared with two in West Coast Berbice. Corentyne has greater stretches of arable land and is the biggest rice-producing district in British Guiana. In addition, there has been a greater development of subsidiary economic activities and a lively commerce from New Amsterdam to Springlands.

Port Mourant is at the centre of this prosperous district with its thriving Indian population, although, since the factory was closed in 1955, there has been acute unemployment and considerable impoverishment. Above the depressed coolie class is a large, relatively well-off middle stratum, consisting not only of drivers and clerks, as in Blairmont, but also of small business men, shop-keepers and contractors, junior civil servants, shop-assistants and teachers, skilled artisans with their own establishments and farmers with five-acre and larger holdings.

This group of persons, of whom only some are directly dependent on the plantation for their livelihood, should, nevertheless, be regarded as a part of the plantation community. They are not completely divorced from the plantation in outlook and interests and are closely related to other residents in numerous ways.[1]

THE WORK CYCLE

The cycle of work follows closely the annual cycle of dry and wet seasons. These seasons are:

February–March	Dry	} 'Spring'
April–August	Wet	
September–October	Dry	} 'Autumn'
November–January	Wet	

The rainfall is heaviest in the middle months of the wet seasons. The two sets of alternate wet and dry seasons enable two crops a year to be grown as compared with one in Trinidad, Barbados, and Jamaica.

The cycle of work begins with the preparation of the field after the harvesting of the previous crop. In the first stage of the preparation, known as flood-fallowing, the field is flooded to a depth of one foot and is kept in that state for about six months. When the water has been drained off the field is ploughed, sometimes with ox-drawn ploughs and sometimes with

[1] For a more detailed description of the two plantations see Smith and Jayawardena, 1959.

tractors. Shovel-men build up the field into alternate rows of beds and ditches and the fork-men then fork the beds and plant the cane in double rows. Shortly afterwards the manuring gang sprinkles lime to counteract the acidity of the soil. The space between the rows of shoots is weeded and 'moulded' by the weeders.

About twelve months after planting the cane is ripe and ready for reaping. Since cane is planted twice each year, there are two annual reaping seasons. The dry foliage of the cane is fired to make reaping easier. The cane is reaped with a cutlass, tied in bundles, and carried to transport punts moored in the canals. 'Mule-boys' in charge of these mule or tractor-drawn punts steer them to the factory.

At the factory the cane is fed into a series of big mills, where it is thoroughly crushed and the resulting dark brown juice is filtered through strainers, heated, and poured into tanks where it is allowed to settle until all impurities have sunk to the bottom. The clarified juice is then poured into vacuum pans and heated again until the water content evaporates and crystals begin to form. The pan-boiler controls the process of crystallization until grains of the required size appear. The sugar is bagged and taken to the riverside docks, where it is loaded into barges which are towed by schooners to Georgetown.

The molasses, the dark brown viscous liquid that remains in the pan after the maximum amount of sugar has been crystallized, is run into large vats where it is fermented and distilled to produce rum.

Other important types of work, subsidiary to the main process of sugar production, are research (chemical and botanical), repair and maintenance of canals, sluices, bridges, railway lines, machines and motors, and medical care, sanitation, and gardening.

Work in the fields begins between six and seven in the morning, and ends usually between four and six. Factory work is carried out in three shifts. Cane-cutters, shovel-men, fork-men, and weeders are paid by 'task', i.e. piece-rate; others are paid at a daily or hourly rate.

THE UNIT OF STUDY

The social unit with which I am concerned is the sugar plantation as exemplified by Blairmont and Port Mourant. It is a constituent unit of Guianese society but can be isolated from it in terms of certain differentiating principles which are of major importance in the structure of the total society. One such factor is the division of labour and the organization of economic activities into various industries. Guianese society can also be differentiated into classes which, for the purposes of this study, may be termed simply upper, middle, and lower. Class differentiation divides persons engaged in sugar production into groups who have similar 'life chances'. By this criterion, the vast majority of persons whose behaviour I shall examine belong to the lower class.

The third important factor is the ethnic differentiation that divides

Guianese into White, Negro, Coloured, Chinese, Indian and Amerindian. This study is almost entirely concerned with Indians who, on the two plantations, constitute respectively about 89 per cent and 99 per cent of the households. Physically and culturally the Indians can be differentiated from the Negroes as well as from the other ethnic groups; they regard themselves as an 'Indian community' and set up several distinguishing criteria. Thus the boundaries of that unit of the wider society investigated in this study can be defined by the demarcations of sugar plantation, lower class and Indian.

These lines of differentiation operate on different levels, that is to say, the groups formed by these several structural principles are not identical. Consequently while much of the social action studied here arises from the interaction of these different planes, it is necessary to keep them conceptually distinct. For structuring by industrial, class, and ethnic principles does not affect all kinds of social activities equally and their operation and relevance in different situations and for different persons may vary. In one situation, a person may act as an 'Indian', aligning himself with plantation, village, and urban Indians, in contradistinction to Whites, Chinese and Negroes; in another context, he may act as a 'labourer' and align himself with Negro labourers, in opposition to the upper classes, Indian and others. Again, in the matter of pay-increases, or the allocation of special funds for welfare, the interests of those concerned in sugar production coincide, as opposed to those of other groups of the society.

Further, within this structure, there is considerable latitude for personal choice.[1] An individual may be able to decide which of these group affiliations he will manipulate to serve his ends. A candidate in an election may exploit now one and now another set of affiliations, depending on the potentialities of the situation. This being so, it is pertinent to question the validity of attempts to freeze an essentially dynamic situation and formulate rigid categories such as the 'plantation society' (based on differentiation in the industrial structure),[2] or a 'proletarian society' (based on differentiation in the class structure), or a 'plural society' (based on differentiation in the ethnic structure).[3] These frameworks are of doubtful value because they necessarily exclude factors that cannot be subsumed in their particular schemes; they ignore the fact of 'cross-cutting membership' in distinct and opposed groups which tends to integrate the total society.[4] Thus class affiliations cut across industrial groups and ethnic affiliations cut across classes. The orientation of labourers to 'bourgeois' values underlines their links with the total society and places limits on the development of a proletarian or a plantation culture. The total form of the social system is distorted by attempts to force it into the rigid framework of a 'plantation', a 'plural' or a 'proletarian' society.

Although the plantation, as a unit, has been isolated from its wider

[1] Firth, 1954, 1955.   [2] Wagley, 1957.   [3] Smith, M. G., 1955.
[4] Fortes, 1953, p. 29; Gluckman, 1954a, p. 67.

context because certain social phenomena can be studied most usefully in terms of relationships within it, this does not mean that all the important relations and values governing behaviour are contained within its limits. In no sense is either Blairmont or Port Mourant an autonomous social system. Factors which operate at the level of the wider social system directly affect the behaviour of the plantation labourers; the persons studied here as plantation residents, labourers, and Indians are also caught up in other and wider relationships.[1]

For example, every labourer of the plantation is a citizen of the Colony of British Guiana, and as such his behaviour is regulated by various government departments. One of these is the Labour Department. Before the growth of trade unions it was to the Labour Department that the labourers turned for help in trade disputes and the Department continues to play an important role in management-labour relations. A few decades ago the Immigration Department, popularly known as the 'Crosby',[2] was in charge of most affairs pertaining to Indians. Other important government departments are the Police Force and the judiciary, which function as the formal media of social control in the local community. The policies and practices of these departments are formulated and regulated at the national level.

The two plantations are parts of the wider structure of the company which owns them both. In recent years the administration of these plantations has been increasingly centralized. Cultivation and employment policies, the degree of mechanization, production targets, etc., are decided in Georgetown, not locally. Management personnel, most of whom are recruited in Great Britain, are promoted, transferred or dismissed by the head offices of the company in Georgetown or London. They participate in the social life of the plantation only to a limited extent, and regard their important relations as operating at the level of the wider society and in kinship and other social groups in Britain. In so far as they occupy positions of power in the organization of the plantation, they constitute an important link between the plantation and the wider society. In the past, when there was closer contact between management and labourers, this relationship would have influenced attitudes and values and, to this extent, have been an agent of social change.

Most labourers are members of a nationally organized trade union, the Man-Power Citizens' Association (M.P.C.A., popularly known as 'Man-Power'). All important agreements relating to wages and working conditions are made at the top level, between the M.P.C.A. and the Sugar Producers' Association (representing the company). Less formally, the

---

[1] I follow R. T. Smith in 'treating the whole of British Guiana as an autonomous unit for the purposes of the present analysis' (Smith, 1956, p. 5).

[2] The 'Crosby' was what Indians in British Guiana called the Immigration Department, after James Crosby, an Immigration Agent-General, who had protected the interests of indentured labourers in the nineteenth century.

union leaders participate actively in the political system of the colony, and their decisions may be influenced by factors that operate at a national rather than a local or plantation level.

Since elections to the Legislative Council are based on universal adult franchise, plantation labourers also participate directly in the political system and are called upon to make decisions of national importance. Because of the scarcity of employment in rural areas, the plans of political parties for economic development are matters of perennial interest. Most labourers support the left-wing People's Progressive Party which consciously aligns itself with socialist parties in other parts of the world. Articles in the P.P.P. journal *Thunder*, or news items over Radio Demerara stimulate considerable discussion of the political situations in Algeria, Kenya, Ghana, Cyprus, and Egypt.

Again, in the social stratification of Guianese society links between the plantation and the wider social system are important. In terms of the Guianese status hierarchy 'plantation labourers' tend to be classified as a group. With certain reservations in respect of the more skilled labourers, the Indian plantation labourers, the coolies, are a very low status group. For instance, the Indians of the rice-growing villages consider the Indian plantation labourers to be disorderly and immoral. The low status of the coolies is due in part to their former status as indentured labourers, in part to the control still exercised over them by management, and in part to their poverty and the slender opportunities available to them for accumulating wealth.

The plantation Indians are also a part of the 'Indian community' of British Guiana. This is a sub-group of the wider society which, in certain sectors of social activity, has its own sub-culture. The principles of recruitment into this group determine the sectors in which this sub-culture prevails. Recruitment to the group is primarily by descent. Phenotypical characteristics are used to differentiate outsiders. In relation to Negroes, skin colour is not a very useful criterion because some Indians are as dark as, if not darker than, some Negroes; emphasis has therefore shifted to texture of hair. But while the Indian group is primarily one of descent, cultural considerations make important modifications. The *dogla* (offspring of an Indian-Negro union) can, if he so wishes, become assimilated into the Indian group; that is, he can freely adopt the behaviour patterns appropriate to being an Indian; he is a Hindu or a Muslim, he marries according to the rites of his Indian religion, and he pays homage to the value of 'being Indian'. Patterns of cultural behaviour can make radical changes in status by descent. This is borne out by the status, intermediate between Indian and Negro, enjoyed by Negro Muslims. It is again reflected in the ambiguous status of the highly Westernized Indian of the upper class who is usually a Christian and does not maintain 'Indian custom'. He too occupies a marginal position in the Indian group; people repeatedly said of certain upper-class Indians, 'Dey nah Indian'.

There is no formal expression of the unity of the Indian community. The British Guiana East Indian Association is no more than a social and cricket club confined largely to the Indian upper and middle status groups. On the other hand, religious organizations are community-wide. These are the Sanatan Dharm Maha Sabha (orthodox Hindu), the United Sad'r Islamic Anjuman (orthodox Muslim), the American Aryan League (reformist Hindu), and the British Guiana Ahmediya Anjuman (reformist Muslim).

The importance of the religious organizations seems to emphasize a division of the Indian community into Hindu and Muslim, and each of the Hindu and Muslim groups into orthodox and reformist. Yet these differences are important only in some contexts. In general it is true to say that the overall tie of 'being Indian' is strong enough to override religious distinctions. The religious organizations provide leadership, advice, and help in many religious and cultural activities. The visits, talks, and sermons of prominent members of the Indian community, as well as the visits of missionaries and 'cultural ambassadors' from India, are major foci of the 'Indian' activities of plantation Indians.

2

Historical and Social Background

THE culture and attitudes of the plantation Indians have been moulded by the experience of their immigrant ancestors. It is necessary, therefore, to discuss briefly those events and processes occurring during the period 1838–1917 which have had a formative influence on present conditions.

THE INDENTURE SYSTEM

The acute shortage of plantation labour caused by Emancipation was met by immigration schemes financed jointly by the planters and the colonial government. After experimenting with immigrants from various countries, the planters and the government settled for Indian coolies as being the most suitable. Between 1838 and 1917, 238,960 Indians were imported, more than two-thirds of whom did not return to India.

An examination of the birth-places of a sample of immigrants for the period 1865–1917[1] shows that 70·3 per cent came from Northwest Province and Oudh,[2] 15·3 per cent from Bihar, and 4·4 per cent from the South Indian Provinces. 83·6 per cent were Hindu and 16·3 per cent Muslim. 13·6 per cent belonged to the higher castes (Brahmin, Kshatriya, etc.), 30·1 per cent to the agricultural castes (Kurmi, Ahir, etc.), 8·7 per cent to the artisan castes (Nonia, Koiri, etc.), and 31·1 per cent to the menial castes (Chamar, Dusad, etc.).

The coolies were imported under what was known as the 'indenture system', which regulated their recruitment, labour contracts, and living conditions. The indenture contract bound the coolies (a) to perform five years' continuous service as plantation labourers, (b) to work seven hours in the field or ten in the factory, (c) to perform five 'tasks' weekly, a task being defined as one day's labour. Able-bodied males were paid one shilling per task, non-able-bodied males and females eightpence. A coolie was required to live on the plantation and each family was entitled to free housing and medical attention. After five years' service the coolie received a certificate of exemption from labour[3] which entitled him to work any-where in the colony. Those who re-indentured themselves received a bounty

---

[1] Smith, 1959.
[2] Later known as the United Provinces, and now as Uttar Pradesh.
[3] That is, compulsory labour in a plantation.

of fifty dollars. After ten years' residence, those who wished to return home were entitled to half their fare.

Breach of indenture (concerning which no provision was made in the contract) was dealt with not by the ordinary civil law, but under the Consolidated Immigration Ordinance (No. 4 of 1864 and amendments). The Ordinance laid down that any coolie who failed to fulfil his indenture obligations could be punished by the courts. A coolie whose performance was unsatisfactory owing to absence or neglect was liable, on the report of the manager to the magistrate, to a fine not exceeding $24.00 or two months' hard labour. The manager who did not pay a coolie his correct wages was not subject to a fine, but the coolie was free to sue him in a civil court or to complain to the Immigration Department. Absence from the plantation for longer than a week without permission constituted 'desertion', an offence punishable by a fine or imprisonment or both. Further, any immigrant found at a distance of more than two miles from the plantation, without a pass from the manager, could be arrested by the police. The number of work days lost by imprisonment for any of these offences was added to the period of indenture.

The effect of the indenture system[1] was to deliver the coolies completely into the power of the manager. It is open to doubt whether the Immigration Ordinance was ever intended to be an equitable regulation of the relations between coolies and planters. Joseph Beaumont, Chief Justice of the Colony, commented:

The ordinary law of master and servant in Demerara is severe enough in all conscience, and unequal enough as between master and servant (to say nothing of the unequal mode of its administration) to satisfy the most exact demands of the former. It is, however, a liberal and just code as compared with what are specifically known as the 'labour laws', i.e. the compulsory and penal provisions of the law for enforcing the immigrants to labour.[2]

Both the formal provisions of the Ordinance and its administration were heavily weighted in favour of the planters. Critics of the system pointed out a number of its injustices, for instance: (a) the rates of pay offered by the recruiters were the maximum that could be earned by a hard-working able-bodied coolie; (b) the manager could not be compelled to offer regular work; (c) there was no mention in the contract of the offence of 'desertion'; (d) criminal sanctions were used to enforce contractual obligations; (e) there was no adequate provision for enforcing the rights of the immigrant (the payment of a just wage and the provision of suitable accommodation and medical facilities).

Moreover managers abused their power. Several observers commented

---

[1] For a detailed analysis of the indenture system in British Guiana see: Amos, 1871, Whitfield, 1872, Harris, c. 1910, Jenkins, 1871, Beaumont, 1871, Des Voeux, 1948, Dalton, 1855, Rodway, 1891–4, Ruhomon, 1939, and Nath, 1950.

[2] Beaumont, op. cit., p. 16.

on the terrible living conditions of the labourers. There were reports of managers 'over-tasking' their labourers and under-paying them. Recalcitrant labourers were taken to court for breach of the labour laws. James Crosby, the Immigration Agent-General, referred to cases of coolies being arrested and gaoled for desertion when on their way to complain to the Immigration Department. It was notoriously difficult for one coolie to give evidence on behalf of another in a case brought to court by the manager. Des Voeux alleged collusion between the magistrates and the managers.[1] Commenting on the Ordinance in his evidence before the Commission of Inquiry of 1870, Crosby concluded, 'An immigrant is totally powerless; that is a general rule.'[2]

Criticism of the indenture system, both in British Guiana and in England, led to the appointment of the Commission of Inquiry of 1870. This was the starting-point for a succession of reforms, but opposition to the system, bred by the earlier abuses, persisted. In the second decade of the twentieth century Congress leaders in India, Gandhi in particular, opposed it and in 1917, in response to repeated demands, the Viceroy imposed a ban on the emigration of coolies.

SOCIAL INTEGRATION OF THE IMMIGRANTS

'Give me my heart's desire in coolies', exclaimed a planter to Trollope, 'and I will make you a million hogsheads of sugar.'[3] In fact the indenture system did give the planters their heart's desire. It ensured them untrammelled freedom to control the lives and services of their coolies and to transform them into an efficient labour force. Accordingly the sugar industry recovered from the set-backs it had suffered during the early decades of the nineteenth century. Changes in the culture of the immigrants inevitably accompanied this process.

The plantation was the main institution through which the Indian immigrants were integrated into Guianese society. Jenkins described the sugar plantation around 1870 as follows:

Take a large factory in Manchester or Birmingham or Belfast, build a wall round it, shut in its working people from all intercourse, save at rare intervals, with the outside world, keep them in absolute heathen ignorance, and get all the work you can out of them, treat them not unkindly, leave their social habits and relations to themselves, as matters not concerning you who make money from their labour, and you would have constituted a little community resembling in no small degree, a sugar estate village in British Guiana.[4]

The complete isolation of the plantation and the coolies was indeed the most striking feature of the social system of the plantation during and even after the indenture period. The Indian Immigration Ordinance made the

---

[1] Des Voeux, op. cit., pp. 113–48.   [2] Quoted by Amos, op. cit., p. 13.
[3] Trollope, 1867. A million hogsheads was roughly the world's production of sugar at the time.   [4] Jenkins, op. cit., p. 95.

coolies a class apart from the rest of the population and tied them down to the plantation. Managements of plantations were responsible for most matters relating to the coolies; the regulation of their affairs by the Immigration Department was largely confined to the registration of marriages and to dealing with complaints about living conditions. There were no trade unions, political parties or other associations to represent them in the wider system.

The powerlessness of the coolie was matched by his low status. He was brought in to fill the vacuum created by the exodus of the emancipated slaves from the plantations. 'Field labour', as Dalton pointed out,[1] constituted the lowest rung in the occupational hierarchy. The reluctance of the Negroes to work on the plantations, attributed by contemporary writers and administrators to their 'laziness', was due rather to their desire to attain a higher status as independent peasant proprietors, which the availability of suitable land at the time made possible.

The coolie succeeded to the slave's status as well as to his lowly-rated occupation. The analogy between slavery and indenture was close, as several contemporary writers noted. The main difference was that indenture took the form of a 'free' contract for a limited period. In this matter public opinion in British Guiana during the indenture period compromised between the ideology of the age of slavery and the new conception of the liberty of the individual of the *laissez-faire* age. The indenture contract was defended as a free and voluntary agreement, and the coolie was despised for his lack of freedom.

Another contributory factor was the culture of the coolies which differed widely from the 'European' culture of Guianese society. Their language was 'outlandish', they knew no English; their clothes were strange and their religion was heathen. They lacked the cultural characteristics valued in the society, and in return the society withheld its rights and privileges from them. Indian culture or 'coolie culture', as it was and is called, became a mark of low status in the eyes of the white upper status group as well as of the coloured and black lower status groups.

However, Jenkins was misinformed in one important particular—that the managers had no interest in the 'social habits and relations' of the coolies. The integration of the coolie in an effective labour force necessitated a reorganization of his extra-labour relations. Several features of Indian culture had to be adapted to the social system of the plantation.

Social Control

One respect in which managers took an interest in the social life of the labourers was in the arbitration and settlement of inter-personal disputes. This was an inevitable corollary of the effective isolation of the coolie from the institutions of the wider society. Management personnel were briefed:

[1] Dalton, op. cit., pp. 255–6.

When complaints are brought to you by the immigrants or labourers against one another, listen patiently to them; inquire into the whole matter, see where the quarrel originated; for if this is done, not only can serious Court cases be avoided (which makes the estate lose so much labour by the people going as witnesses) but a better feeling is established between the employers and the employees.[1]

The judicial functions of the manager were a well-established feature. Most managers were Justices of the Peace, but the manager's court did not administer the law of the colony; rather it enforced the rules of management and in inter-personal disputes dispensed, to use a term employed by Weber, a kind of 'kadi-justice', i.e. 'judgments rendered in terms of concrete ethical or other practical valuations'.[2] The manager's court was held at regular intervals, presided over by the manager himself or a senior official as his deputy; a driver or a rural constable acted as court orderly. The plaintiff laid his complaint and, if there was a *prima facie* case, the manager summoned the defendant. He called witnesses, and allowed the contending parties to argue the case. If, after sifting the evidence, he was able to apportion the blame, he gave his verdict. If, as frequently happened, the issues were not clear-cut, he warned both parties to 'behave'. If the issues were serious he advised the plaintiff to take the matter to the magistrate's court. On some plantations the labourers were not expected to take their disputes to the magistrate's court until the manager had first considered the dispute and given the plaintiff permission 'to take out a summons'.

The manager had powerful sanctions at his command. He could shift a man's residence from one part of the plantation to another or expel him; he could suspend a labourer from work and levy fines. With these powers he settled marital disputes, quarrels between labourers, complaints about assault, nuisance, defamation, and larceny. He sanctioned marriages, effected divorces, divided property, executed wills and witnessed sales of land and cattle.

Caste

One of the first features of the traditional culture to be modified by the integration of the coolies into the social system of the plantation was caste. Caste restrictions impeded the efficient deployment of the labour force. Managers valued their coolies primarily as labourers and were indifferent to other considerations. A contemporary rating of castes according to their qualities as labourers evaluated Ahir, Chamar and Dusad as 'best labourers', Kshatriya and Kahar as 'good labourers', and Brahmins and Bania as 'worthless'.[3]

Several accounts refer to the 'pernicious influence' of the high castes on the lower. High-caste coolies were suspected of being ring-leaders in strikes and other disturbances. Their influence, parallel to the authority of

---

[1] *The Overseer's Manual*, 1887, p. 38.   [2] Weber, 1958, p. 216.
[3] Comins, 1893, p. 79.

management and sometimes competing with it, was an obstacle to the efficient administration of the coolies.

Managers did not give the caste hierarchy the consideration necessary to maintain it as a system. They divided the coolies into gangs, made them work next to each other and appointed persons to positions of authority irrespective of caste. They housed the coolies cheek by jowl in long barracks and accommodated them together in the hospital. Coolies shared the same water supply, bathed in the same canal and used the same latrines.

The industrial organization of the plantation labourers, which allocated status and rewards according to achievement, was basically incompatible with the ascriptive caste hierarchy. All had equal access to economic resources which were distributed on the basis of labour and skill. Lucrative positions, privileges, and favours were accorded to those whom the management could trust. The rights of the higher castes and the duties of the lower received no support from the administrative system. In these circumstances caste restrictions and superiorities persisted only in an attenuated form. In the latter half of the indenture period several writers noted the decline of the caste system.[1] These changes were, of course, gradual, but eventually it was impressed on the labourers themselves that their most important rights and duties derived from their status in the labour organization.

Other factors contributing to the decline of the caste system may be noted in passing.[2] A severe shortage of women right up to the end of the indenture period made the maintenance of caste endogamy difficult. Since the immigrants came in as individuals and not in groups, there was no check on claims to caste status. It is not possible to assess the extent to which caste changes occurred in transit from India, but it is thought to be considerable. For this reason the legitimacy of high-caste status has been challenged. Further, the gradual integration of the plantation Indians into the wider society introduced them into a world of business men, civil servants, professionals, Negroes and Chinese. Here Indians of wealth and high occupational status gained prestige, irrespective of caste.

At present caste is found in an atrophied form. Defining a caste system in Stevenson's terms,[3] one may say that there is no caste system in the plantations or, probably, throughout British Guiana. For the Guianese Indian, caste is neither an endogamous nor a commensal group and has no connotations of ritual purity or pollution. In the Blairmont and Port Mourant samples, less than a fifth of the Hindu marriages are caste endogamous. Caste is of marginal importance in the selection of spouses as compared with occupation, wealth, and education.[4] The offspring of an inter-caste marriage belong to the father's caste.

---

[1] Bronkhurst, 1883, p. 286; Comins, op. cit., p. 79; Singh, 1925, p. 13.
[2] For a further discussion of caste among the Guianese Indians see Smith and Jayawardena, 1959.
[3] Stevenson, 1954.   [4] Smith and Jayawardena, 1959.

The only occasions on which social behaviour reflects caste distinctions are during those orthodox Hindu rituals in which Brahmins occupy a privileged status. However, these privileges are increasingly challenged by the Hindu reformist movements. An egalitarian ideology prevalent among plantation labourers is also antagonistic to caste distinctions and a person who claims caste superiority, at least in public, offends the norms of propriety. Further, to be 'modern' and 'progressive' are positive values. Caste pride has, therefore, tended to become out-of-date. About a sixth of the Hindu household heads in Blairmont and Port Mourant did not know what their caste was; many others arrived at this knowledge after much speculation and did not appear diffident about guessing at a low caste.

Except in the case of a Brahmin priest, caste is not an important determinant of social status. But a high caste can add to, and a low caste detract from, the prestige of a status achieved on other grounds. A vague sense of pride attaches to being born of a high caste, akin to the English concept of 'gentle birth'. But the influence of caste on prestige is associated only with the extremes of the range, i.e., Brahmin and Kshatriya, and Chamar and Dusad; in the middle range caste neither adds to nor detracts from prestige. It is probable that most of those who did not know what their caste was belonged to this middle range. Their caste was socially meaningless and was gradually forgotten.

Kinship[1]

Another feature of Indian culture to be affected was kinship, although it should be noted that factors external to the plantation have both modified and perpetuated the changes brought about by plantation conditions.[2]

It seems unlikely that the joint family was a characteristic of the social strata in India to which the majority of immigrants belonged. A three-generation stem family or a nuclear family, characterized by a strong solidarity based on the unquestioned authority of the father, appears to have been the norm. Early arranged marriages and the economic dependence of adult sons on their father tended to reinforce this pattern.

But in British Guiana new residential arrangements, the changed economic basis of the domestic group, and the substitution of the manager's control for that of the village elders contributed to the establishment of norms more consonant with the plantation.

For instance, in regulating the lives of their labourers, managers acted in terms of their own cultural norms. They housed one nuclear family in each dwelling and provided new accommodation for the children when they got married, usually in another part of the plantation. This was deliberate policy, for they wished to eliminate tensions arising from the

---

[1] For a fuller account of family and kinship among Guianese Indians see Smith and Jayawardena, 1959, and Jayawardena, 1960 and 1962.

[2] It is likely that the immigrants too came from a changing society. For an outline of traditional kinship norms see Dube, 1954, and Marriott, 1955.

difficult position of the resident daughter-in-law. As a rule, no married couple was allowed to reside in the parental home for longer than a few years.

The power of the father in the family was circumscribed to the extent that he was no longer the sole trustee of the economic resources of the domestic group. Adult sons and wives could evade his control in that they had access to economic resources and accommodation that were beyond his control.

Lastly, the manager was the arbitrator in all inter-personal disputes, and his solutions tended to be in terms of the norms of his own culture. He paid attention to the complaints of wives, sons, and daughters-in-law against the husband/father and, if he felt that the man was behaving 'unreasonably', reprimanded him and so limited his authority. Thus the manager's intervention tended to rearrange the domestic relations of the Indians in accordance with Guianese ('European') patterns.

These are some of the influences that have helped to make the Indian family what it is today—nuclear in structure, with considerable though lessened paternal pre-eminence and authority, a greater freedom for sons in the disposal of their earnings, a considerable liberty for children in the choice of spouses, and a temporary extended family phase when the married son lives with his father until he finds his own house.

In the past most marriages were contracted between persons of different plantations, and residence tended to be virilocal. This practice would have resulted in a system of localized patrilineal groups were it not for the fact that migration was prevalent, especially between plantations, as people went in search of work and more congenial conditions. Changes of residence were effected chiefly through matrilateral and affinal links, and there is reason to believe that the maintenance of the custom of marrying out is related to the advantage of having contacts with other plantations. With fewer employment opportunities in rural areas, as well as the increasing freedom for individual choice and romantic attachment, the practice of marrying out is declining.

No kinship group wider than the nuclear or three-generation stem family has any effective or exclusive functions. The kinship system is bilateral and, with the increasing adoption of Guianese terminology and usages, is rapidly losing its traditional patrilineal emphasis. This wider group of kindred is known as the 'family'. Its composition varies widely with individual persons and circumstances. One person's 'family' reveals a wide patrilateral spread, another's a matrilateral spread; one person's 'family' is four generations deep, another's only two. The extent and structure of each person's definition of his 'family' is a function of how he came to settle on the plantation and how long he has been resident there.

Relations within the wider group of kindred are kept alive by visits and co-operation at weddings and funerals. Kinsmen are expected to help one

CSGP C

another and live in harmony, but they are not obliged to do so, and refusal to honour kinship obligations meets with little public criticism. The 'family' performs few functions distinct from those of friends and neighbours. The roles assigned to certain classes of kin in traditional ceremonies are preferably performed by them, but there is a remarkable elasticity in the interpretation of who falls into the appropriate category. A perfectly acceptable ceremony can be performed with friends standing in for kin. Friends are as important as kin in primary groups.

There is a widespread use of such kinship terms as 'uncle', 'auntie', *bhai* (brother), *betta* (son), and *betti* (daughter) in addressing social equals. By this means the whole local community is likened to a group of kin undifferentiated except by age and sex. Behaviour in this community of kin is governed by the same values of mutual respect and co-operation as obtain between fellow-labourers, except that a special deference is due to the older generation and a certain restraint towards women. One may go further and state that the use of a kinship term is one means of establishing equality of status, as is witnessed by the use of the term 'comrade' as a fashionable alternative.

Religion

During the nineteenth century Christian missionaries tried to persuade planters to help in the conversion of the coolies. Managers showed no enthusiasm, however, and gave little support to the British Guiana Coolie Mission and other similar organizations. The missionaries made little headway, for the coolies were said to be remarkably impervious to the new faith.[1]

It seems, however, that traditional religions were not organized until the last two or three decades of the nineteenth century when, as Comins observed,[2] there appears to have been a 'religious revival'. This was marked by the building of Hindu temples and mosques, which presumes some degree of organization. In time managements stepped in to control such activities on plantations, offering in exchange certain favours and amenities. They provided material and some labour for building and repairing temples and mosques, stipends and free quarters for priests, and they recognized festival days as holidays. It was probably managements that persuaded the coolies to conduct their religious activities through associations, with subscriptions, elected committees, and parliamentary procedure for the conduct of meetings. Management helped in keeping accounts, approved appointments to offices and sanctioned the decisions of committees. Elections, minutes, and other association activities were open to scrutiny by management, which also ensured that the associations confined themselves to religious matters.

Today most plantations have organizations of Hindus and Muslims, known as the Sanatan Dharm Sabha and the Sunnatwal Jamaat respec-

[1] Bronkhurst, 1883, pp. 459–60.   [2] Comins, op. cit., pp. 18, 81.

tively, which are backed by management. These associations follow, with certain modifications, the basic doctrines and practices of the Vaishnavite and Sunni versions of Hinduism and Islam.

Cultural changes have made the Guianese Indians receptive to Hindu and Islamic reformist ideas. The reformist Hindu Arya Samaj and Muslim Ahmediya movements stand for modifications and reinterpretations of the traditional beliefs and practices according to more rationalistic canons. At present these movements, also based on voluntary associations, are significant for the enthusiasm rather than the number of their followers. But their proselytizing fervour has confronted rural Indians with issues of 'unrighteous' Brahmin privileges and 'superstitious' traditional practices.

Controversy between the orthodox and reformist associations is one of the main features of religious activity. In Blairmont orthodox associations successfully enlisted management support in preventing the formation of reformist associations in the plantation. Reformist converts join associations in the villages. In Port Mourant reformists were tolerated and are more successful.

Religious activities take two forms. There are the communal festivals organized by the orthodox associations, the Phagwa (Holi) of the Hindus and the Eid of the Muslims. Public participation in these festivals has declined during the last decade and they are increasingly celebrated by smaller groups of neighbours and friends, more on the lines of the *puja* of the Hindus and the Koran *shereef* of the Muslims. These are devotional meetings organized by a household head in his home and conducted by a priest. Close kin and friends are invited to participate not only in the rites but also in the meal or refreshment that follows.

There is no tension between Hindus and Muslims. A tacit agreement not to convert each other and to avoid religious controversy makes cooperation between the associations possible when the situation demands it. Hindus and Muslims attend each other's religious ceremonies freely, and in formal discussions certain precepts believed to be common to both religions are emphasized. For example, it is said that both worship the same God under different names. The basis of this rapprochement is the assertion that both Hindus and Muslims are Indians, in contradistinction to Negroes and Whites, and that their religions are Indian, in contradistinction to Christianity. Hinduism and Islam are regarded as alternative ways of being Indian. A close study of their respective customs reveals that a considerable degree of convergence and syncretism has developed.

Out of 379 households in the Blairmont sample 70·6 per cent were Orthodox Hindus, 3·0 per cent were reformist Hindus, 18·7 per cent were Orthodox Muslims, 2·4 per cent were reformist Muslims, and 5·3 per cent were Christians. Out of 205 households in the Port Mourant sample 69·7 per cent were Orthodox Hindus, 10·7 per cent were reformist Hindus, 10·8 per cent were Orthodox Muslims and 8·8 per cent were Christians; there were no reformist Muslims.

Indian Culture

The integration of Indians into Guianese society created avenues for outside influences in response to which the traditional culture changed in several respects. The change, although it developed more rapidly in some sectors of the culture, was not haphazard.

Two types of change may be distinguished. The first, which may be described as 'creolization',[1] consisted of the substitution of creole for traditional customs. For example, in dress, household furniture and decoration, secular celebrations and material prestige symbols, the Indians have rapidly taken to creole patterns. More important is the transformation of Hindi and Urdu into esoteric languages used almost solely in religious rituals and in traditional wedding songs. Priests often deliver a short sermon in Hindi after a *puja* but translate it into English for the benefit of the congregation. The language of daily use is the dialect of English used by other rural Guianese, *taki-taki*. It can be safely estimated that nine-tenths of those under the age of thirty-five do not understand Hindi. Urban cultural organizations which, in recent times, have re-established contact with corresponding bodies in India have failed in attempts to start Hindi schools in rural areas. Another striking example of creolization is the giving up of cremation and the adoption of burial and of the rural Negro custom of the wake.

The other type of change arose from an overt refusal to give up a traditional custom while, simultaneously, modifying it in certain directions. Considerations of time and work schedules, for example, cause traditional weddings to be held on Sundays; the priest who is asked to select the most auspicious day for a wedding selects the most auspicious Sunday. The availability of cheap motor transport enables the bridegroom and his retinue to visit the bride and return home on the same day, and so shortens the long drawn-out traditional ceremony; but the custom of arriving in some form of transport is maintained. It is the adherence to the custom that is important, not its preservation in its authentic form.

The meaning of a custom may be forgotten, and conflicting reasons may be advanced to explain it. Some, which were quite certainly acquired in British Guiana, are believed to be 'old India custom'; some rituals and ceremonies reflect social relations that are no longer important. The social significance of these customs thus derives from the fact that in Guianese society they are identified as 'Indian', whether or not they are authentic, and whether or not the social relations they symbolize are important. Performance of the traditional customs stamps the actors as Indians, and

[1] In a study of the acculturation of Indians and Negroes in British Guiana (Skinner, 1955) Dr E. P. Skinner uses the term 'Englishification'. I have preferred the term 'creolization' in order to distinguish the Guianese variant of 'English culture' from other variants. The reader is referred to his study for a detailed account of creole customs which have been adopted by Indians. See also Skinner, 1960.

few are concerned with anything except this symbolic value. People are ignorant of or indifferent to variations in the same ritual performed by different priests or to mistakes in such performances. What matters is that an Indian is expected to organize and attend such rituals. They establish his position as a full member of the Indian community. In fact most Indian religious occasions tend to be also convivial gatherings. One way of entertaining friends is to organize a reading of a holy text followed by a meal. It may be noted in passing that until recently no other form of communal activity was permitted in plantations.

Thus while several items of the traditional culture, such as dress, language, cremation, and other festivals and ceremonies have fallen into desuetude, those that have been retained, and in some cases even elaborated, serve as media for maintaining and expressing the solidarity of the Indian community vis-à-vis other ethnic groups. The problem of why some ceremonies (e.g. the *puja*) rather than others (e.g. *Deevali*) were 'selected' for this purpose falls outside the scope of this study.

The creolization of the coolie was never at any stage forced by official authorities, yet there was much informal pressure to change. First, 'English' customs had, in the eyes of all Guianese, a great deal of prestige. The upwardly mobile coolie, like his Negro and Chinese counterparts, acquired these customs. Second, there was a growing realization that conformity to 'English' customs, values, and beliefs brought certain advantages. For example, jobs as school teachers were open mainly to Christians since most schools were controlled by Christian missions. Moreover, high-status groups regarded the deviant customs of the coolies as 'indecent' and 'backward'. The low status accorded to traditional Indian culture provided another incentive to creolization.

A tendency to depreciate the traditional culture is becoming common among the plantation Indians themselves, chiefly among upwardly mobile elements. It is to be expected, therefore, that the traditional culture will be found mainly among those of a low status, i.e. the labourers. High-status Indians are more creolized; many are Christians, and very few participate in traditional ceremonies and rituals. Nevertheless, high-status Indians maintain their affiliation with the Indian group up to a point. Their intermediate position is expressed, in part through reformist religious activities and in part through cultural forms recently imported from India, for example, song recitals, exhibitions of classical dancing, concerts, charity fairs, etc. These activities are more genteel, can be readily distinguished from traditional customs, and are therefore not associated with coolie culture.

Changes in the Plantation System

The existence of the manager's court indicates that the plantation used to be a less rationalized and bureaucratic organization than it is at present. The manager's autocratic power was exercised through a paternalistic role.

He was invited to be present at weddings and religious festivals and usually accepted. He lent wood for the erection of marriage tents and assigned a labour gang to build up the *Holi* pyre. Further, labourers were allotted land to plant rice and vegetables and pastures to raise cattle. Shops, schools, and temples were built on the plantation. In many respects the plantation resembled a self-sufficient village.

The reform of the indenture system and its eventual abolition in 1917 changed the position of the coolies. The government became increasingly responsible for their welfare. The isolation of plantation residents and the manager's power over them were progressively reduced as they became absorbed into the wider society.

After 1917 the number of coolies whose position was regulated by the Indian Immigration Ordinance became progressively less as creole-born generations became full citizens. Constitutional changes enfranchised an increasing number of coolies and brought them into closer relations of competition and co-operation with other ethnic groups. In the last two decades political parties and trade unions have attempted to become their representatives.

These developments have affected the social structure of the plantation; ties between management and labourers have weakened, and those between labourers and other social groups outside the plantation have developed, as a consequence of greater government control and the growth of political parties, trade unions, and other associations. An effective emphasis of class interests by these organizations has considerably reduced the paternalistic power of the manager.

The character of management has changed apace. New organizational methods and standards of efficiency have led to an increasing bureaucratization. In 1870 there were 157 plantations, but today these have been merged into 16 controlled by two companies, with a consequent coordination and standardization of policies. The autocratic manager of the nineteenth century has gradually been replaced by a salaried official who is bound by explicit terms of appointment and by periodic instructions from a central head office. The manager's personal control of the social relations of his labourers is giving way to bureaucratically organized welfare schemes drawn up by 'experts'. Besides, the recognition of trade unions has institutionalized differences of interest between management and labourers and lessened the paternalistic responsibility of the manager. In fact technological developments tend to make large concentrations of resident labourers unnecessary. The policy of managements is to mechanize, to reduce the number of residents for whom they are responsible, and to depend increasingly on the more impersonal relations of the labour market.

These processes are producing a new social order which, however, is not without its teething troubles, for the experiences of previous generations persist as traditions of the present. While, on the one hand, the labourers are asserting their position in a nation-wide class of 'poor people', they have not relinquished their claims to protection by management from the vicissitudes of the labour market. Again, while managers have renounced their former obligations to look after their labourers, they have not relinquished their claims to authority in extra-industrial affairs.

The past has moulded the present in other ways too. The isolation of the coolies during the indenture period helped to form Indian group-consciousness. The injustices of the past survive in the common saying: 'A-we coolie people proper punish',[1] which is repeated over and over again both as comment on a particular state of affairs and as a generalization about the nature of life. The tradition of having been oppressed has engendered a suspicion of authority and the upper classes which reinforces the solidarity of the Indian labouring group. The autonomy of the plantation has bred a strong sense of attachment to it, for to the coolies the plantation has been not merely private property or a place of work, but a land from which they drew their sustenance in many ways besides wage labour. They collected timber and planted fruit-trees on unused land and fished in the flooded fields and canals. Management set aside lands for their rice-fields and pastures and employed 'cow-minders' to look after their cattle. Their parents were buried in the plantation cemetery and their children were born in the plantation hospital.

The withdrawal of many of these concessions in the name of modernization has created some perplexity; their replacement by the cricket clubs and sewing classes of welfare schemes has not been readily accepted. Ironically, the tough and paternalistic manager of the old regime had a surer sense of the needs of a labourer than the democratic welfare workers of the present. The manager's 'welfare' of the old days allowed the labourers a measure of autonomy in their personal affairs which is absent in the neatly drawn rules of modern welfare schemes.

Increase of population and technological innovations have caused a scarcity of work on the plantations which is not compensated by the growth of new industries. Most labourers feel that since they 'born and grow' on the plantation, management 'must responsible'. In the past they obeyed the manager, and the manager looked after them. But while the duties of a manager in an industry increasingly rationalized can be re-defined by a circular from Georgetown, the attitude of the labourers that management owes them a duty of care dies hard. These attitudes are only gradually being replaced by others more consonant with the changing political and economic structure of the society.

[1] The word 'punish' is used in the sense of 'suffer'.

3

Social Stratification

SINCE the plantation is essentially an industrial organization certain of its characteristics are of primary importance. First it is a capitalist enterprise and thus much of its activity is governed by the need to make profits, and market conditions affect the life of the community in many ways. Second, the plantation brings together several hundred persons in regular relationships. Third, the operation of the enterprise requires the co-ordination of a variety of agricultural, engineering, and mechanical acti-vities. These characteristics are crucial foci in the social system of the plantation.[1]

For instance economic considerations are a basic determinant of group membership. A distinctive feature of the plantation as a local unit is that recruitment to it is based on labour; a person's claim to membership depends on whether he is of use to the system of sugar production. The head of almost every family in the plantation (and in families with a female head, her son) works for it. The only exceptions are young children, some wives, old men past working age, shop-keepers and a few who ply trades essential to plantation life such as barbers, tailors, and priests.

Unlike the local government authority of a village, management is not primarily concerned with the welfare of the plantation residents or the administration of their affairs, but with the production of sugar at an economical cost. It therefore provides residential rights and other facilities only to those who, in return, offer their labour. Anyone who refuses to do so is liable to eviction because management owns the land and most of the houses.

The relationship of the labourer to the productive organization is there-fore the basis of the social system of the plantation. The complex division of labour and the system of occupational roles that this entails provide the framework for social action within the community. In the social system of the plantation the occupational system corresponds to the kinship systems

[1] See Mintz and Wolf, 1957, for a discussion of the general characteristics of the plantation as an economic organization. The plantations of British Guiana seem to be a transitional type between two ideal types of large-scale agricultural pro-duction: the 'hacienda' and the 'plantation'. The plantations of British Guiana in the nineteenth century had many of the characteristics of the hacienda. The changes discussed in the last chapter have tended to make them approximate to the 'plantation'.

of primitive societies. There is a close link between a person's role in the occupational system and his roles in other fields of social action. For instance, a person's role as a member of the local Indian community has to be adapted to his role as an employee. In other words, an Indian who is a plantation resident can perform only those actions of his Indian role which do not conflict with his rights and duties as an employee. The changes in Indian culture described in Chapter 2 are partly the result of this situation.

The organization of plantation residents as a labour force creates several economic interests common to them all. Apart from the shop-keepers and the Junior Staff, they all perform similar kinds of work, earn wages varying only within narrow limits, depend on the vicissitudes of sugar prices and the labour market, and are subordinate to the same officials. These common economic interests place them all in the same class.[1] Their low income, common style of life, and the low evaluation of manual labour place them all in the same social status. To this extent plantation labourers may be described as a homogeneous social group. However, the validity of this generalization depends on the level of analysis. It is adequate if one is concerned with the total society, but a sharper focus on the local group reveals lines of internal differentiation.

As part of the local community the labourers are related to other classes and status groups. Management personnel may be described as belonging to an 'upper' or 'employer' status group and the Junior Staff as belonging largely to a white collar 'middle' status group. The local community can thus be regarded as a hierarchy of status groups with managerial personnel at the top, the Junior Staff in the middle and the labourers at the bottom. By social stratification I refer to this hierarchy. Relations between the classes will be discussed in the following chapter.

OCCUPATIONAL STRUCTURE

The basis of social stratification in the plantation is the occupational structure. Occupational roles can be classified into supervisory, clerical, and labouring, providing the following chart:

Supervisory	Clerical	Labouring
Manager	Accountant	Pan-boiler
Overseer	Book-keeper	Electrician
Engineer	Store-keeper	Mill-hand
Housing Officer	Typist, etc.	Boiler-attendant

[1] In this study I follow Weber's definitions of 'class' and 'status' (Weber, 1958, pp. 180–95). Contemporary sociologists have combined the concepts Weber differentiated and speak of 'social class', e.g. Warner, Meeker, and Eels, 1949, Schumpeter, 1955, and Parsons, 1954. However, I have retained Weber's distinction because it is useful in analysing systems of social stratification in multi-racial societies. Unfortunately this also leads me to use the term 'middle status' where these writers would speak of 'middle class'.

Supervisory	*Labouring*
Chemist	Mechanic
Doctor	Tractor-operator
Welfare Officer	Carpenter
Field Clerk	Porter
Driver	Cane-cutter
Foreman, etc.	Shovel-man
	Fork-man
	Weeder
	Watchman
	Dock-worker, etc.

This classification distorts the real situation slightly. The Chief Electrician performs supervisory duties as well as tasks which require his manual skill. The inclusion of 'doctor' among supervisory roles is questionable, but one can argue that the main duty of the plantation doctor is to see whether a labourer is fit to work or requires sick leave and compensation.

Supervisory Roles

Supervisory roles co-ordinate the various activities of the productive organization. The Administrative Manager is at the apex of a pyramidal system of authority. He receives general directives from the head offices of the company in Georgetown but has considerable latitude in interpreting them. His main duty is to see that the quota of sugar expected from the plantation is produced, and to do this within the budget allowed him. He plans current expenditure, the numbers to be employed and the extension or reduction of the area under cultivation. He co-ordinates the three main departments of plantation work—the field, the factory, and the office. Each of these departments is supervised by a manager who is directly responsible to him.

The Field Manager supervises the cultivation of sugar. The rota of planting and fallowing, the varieties of cane to be planted, the kinds of manures and insecticides used, the time to cut the cane, and general irrigation problems are his concern. Under him are two or more Assistant Field Managers, each in charge of a section of the plantation.

Once the labour gangs have been deployed, an overseer is put in charge of each gang, who assigns their tasks to individual labourers and supervises their work. The driver (a foreman of field labour) helps him to allot the tasks and to price the work. The driver operates at the point where the decisions of management are passed on to the labourers. For example, the Assistant Field Manager tells the overseer that drains are to be dug to certain specifications; the overseer communicates this order to the driver and, with his advice, estimates the number of labourers required and the price to be paid for the work, e.g. so many cents per foot of drain. The overseer is responsible for the quality of the job as a whole, the driver supervises each individual labourer, noting the amount of work done and the wages due to him; the overseer checks the driver's accounts each evening.

This system gives the driver a great deal of authority and influence. However, his duties are concurrent with those of the overseer and much depends on whether relations between them are amicable. In any dispute between the driver and the labourers, management, on principle, upholds the driver.

The Factory Manager co-ordinates the various departments of the factory and steps up or cuts down production in accordance with the directives of the Administrative Manager. The factory operates only for a part of the year, during the 'grinding seasons', i.e. when the cane is cut. The periods between crops are devoted to repair and maintenance during which time unskilled labourers obtain only occasional employment. The Factory Manager has two or more engineers and several overseers to supervise the detailed application of his instructions. The foremen of the factory correspond to the drivers of field gangs. Each subdivision of factory work —mechanical, electrical, and diesel—has a foreman in charge of it. Foremen, like drivers, are recruited from among the labourers.

A laboratory attached to the factory is in the charge of a chemist. He is responsible for seeing that the sugar and rum produced are of the required standard.

Clerical Roles

The office prepares the weekly wage-lists and keeps the accounts and records of the plantation. This branch of work is supervised by the Office Manager, helped by the Assistant Accountant. Below them is the Head Book-keeper who supervises the work of the clerks with the help of three Senior Assistants. Some clerks are assigned to the factory and work under the senior clerks there—the Chief Time-keeper and the Store-keeper. Junior clerks do not have fixed or specialized tasks and are shifted from one type of job to another according to the exigencies of work.

There is a precise sense of rank although (or because) only a few positions are formally plotted in the hierarchy. Once tasks have been assigned, the elaborate division of labour, the settled routine of work and this consciousness of rank regulate behaviour in the office to a high degree, and the spatial arrangement of the office reflects this. The clerks occupy a large room, a section of which is partitioned off for the Office Manager who exercises a silent supervision through its glass panels. Normally the Head Book-keeper and the Senior Assistants have permanent desks. The desk of the former is close to the partition facing the centre of the room and within easy call of the Office Manager. The junior clerks sit wherever they can most conveniently carry out the tasks at hand and are not given permanent desks. This structure is also reflected in the behaviour between clerks, especially in the use of 'Mister' or a first name, and in the familiarity or respect with which one may address another.

Labouring Roles

The labourers—the largest group in the occupational structure—can be divided into field labourers and factory labourers. The types of skill that each category brings into the productive process are different and are, to some extent, evaluated differently.

Field labourers are engaged in the cultivation of cane and factory labourers are engaged in the processing of sugar. In Port Mourant there are now no factory labourers and only a small workshop for repairing the mechanized equipment used in the field remains.

Field Gangs

The following table gives the size of the field labour force of each plantation, with its division into gangs. The figures include both plantation and village residents.[1]

TABLE 4

Composition of the Field Labour Force

	Blairmont 1956	*Port Mourant* 1957
General Purposes Gang	64	178
General Maintenance Gang	319	284
Shovel Gang	233	98
Male Weeding Gang	49	125
Female Weeding Gang	193	390
Cane-cutting Gang	319	662
Cane Transport Gang	179	93
Field Mechanic Gang	57	97
	1,413	1,927

Except in the shovel and weeding gangs, plantation residents and villagers work in the same gangs. At a rough estimate about 57 per cent of the Blairmont field labour force and about 80 per cent of the Port Mourant field labour force are resident labourers. There are several reasons for the differences in the size of gangs: (*a*) Port Mourant has no factory and cultivates a much larger area than Blairmont; (*b*) it is more highly mechanized than Blairmont, using more drain-cutters and tractors; and (*c*) gangs are fluid groups and many registered under one gang may in fact be employed in another type of work. The difference in the proportions of resident labourers is a reflection of the greater prosperity of the Corentyne region which is therefore less dependent on plantations.

The composition of gangs varies according to sex, age, and ethnic origin. Attendance in the female weeding gang fluctuates a great deal. The most regular workers are usually widows and women separated from their husbands. Mothers of young families give up working until the eldest child is old enough to look after the household, and even then various household

[1] I am indebted to the office staffs of Blairmont and Port Mourant for these figures.

duties and problems may from time to time prevent them from working.[1]

Another gang, composed entirely of old women is the 'Granny gang', who weed the lawn of the senior staff compound. It is part of a larger, more composite gang known as the 'General Maintenance gang' or the 'Creole gang'. A few women work in the male gangs, manuring, baling punts, carrying drinking water, etc.

Age, or rather physical prowess, provides another difference. The male weeding gangs usually consist of boys and the less fit adult males. Most cane-cutters are young and able-bodied for few continue to cut cane after they have reached their forties. The shovel and forking gangs contain a high proportion of middle-aged men. Several old men are employed as watchmen and rangers.

Ethnic affiliation is another relevant difference. Most of the Negro residents of Blairmont work in the factory. In fact about half the factory labour force is Negro. Many of these men come from across the river or from the neighbouring village of Ithaca. Conversely, the majority of the field labour force is Indian. To interpret this as occupational specialization is to freeze into a static category what is essentially a fluid situation. The indentured immigrants were put to work in the fields while the factory relied on skilled Negro artisans. But in recent times Indians have been acquiring technical skills and soon the ethnic composition of the factory will correspond to the ethnic composition of the area. In this, as in other respects, Port Mourant exhibits trends that are incipient in Blairmont. Almost all the workshop labourers in Port Mourant are Indians and most of the skilled labourers in the Port Mourant factory were Indian too.

Cane-cutting gangs in Blairmont have a high proportion of Negroes compared with Indians. One reason might be that Negroes are, on an average, more robust and able to stand the rigours of cane-cutting. But here too scarcity of other kinds of field labour is compelling many Indians to cut cane, which is probably the only kind of field labour not affected by mechanization. In Port Mourant cane-cutting gangs are composed mainly of Indians.

The gang is a group organized by management, and membership is obtained by being accepted as an employee. The number of persons and the work assigned to each gang depend on production requirements. At the present time work is scarce, and though names are in the books as belonging to this or that gang there is no assurance of work. Usually the driver informs the labourers, either the day before or early in the morning when they gather at the locomotive stop, that work is available. During the grinding season, when work is plentiful, a labourer knows how many days of work lie ahead. On some days there is work for everyone and on others only for a few. The composition of the gang therefore fluctuates and this fluctuation is increased by mobility from gang to gang. A labourer who works in a cane-cutting gang during one crop may prefer to work in the

[1] See Jayawardena, 1962, for a discussion of this topic.

shovel gang in the next and in the cane transport gang in the third. Transfer from gang to gang requires the permission of management which, however, disapproves of gang-changing.

Other factors can cause inter-gang mobility. In a large plantation agricultural requirements vary from week to week and within limits are unpredictable. Unlike in the factory, it is impossible to work out all details and to keep a fixed schedule. One field may require more weeding than another, a sudden deluge of rain may cause postponement of cane-cutting, and ploughing a field may take longer than was expected. Although management does make plans for the deployment of the labour force at the beginning of the crop, it has to make several changes and readjustments in the course of the season. Shovel-men may be used for forking beds and cane-cutters for digging drains. Since most field labour occupations are unskilled it is not difficult for a labourer to work in a variety of gangs nor for management to re-deploy them. As a result most labourers have worked in several branches of field labour and are well acquainted with the nature of work and working conditions in the plantation.

The gang is thus not a group formed by the labourers to meet a need for co-operative effort. Indeed reciprocity or co-operation are not required in most types of field labour. In the formal organization of the gang each labourer is an independent individual. His task for the day is assigned to him individually and his payment is agreed between himself and the management, within the framework of minimum wage rates.

This is the *formal* structure of labour relations. It is, of course, not the whole picture. There is an 'informal' structure[1] which will be discussed at the end of this chapter.

Factory Labourers

The occupational structure of the factory is more complex than that of the field. All that will be attempted here is a brief outline, emphasizing some of its distinctive features.

The most important differentiation in the group of factory workers is that between skilled and unskilled. Skilled labourers include pan-boilers, electricians, welders, mechanics, cane-hoist drivers, distillers, blacksmiths, carpenters, etc. Unskilled labourers include boiler and mill attendants, porters, sweepers, etc. These latter are comparable to the unskilled field labourers. The influx of Indians into the factory, many of them formerly field workers, is a recent phenomenon in Blairmont. The regularity of factory employment is an attraction for many, even though the piece-rates in some types of field labour may be higher. The majority of skilled labourers in the factory are Negro and many of the Indian skilled labourers come from outside the plantation. The plantation-born Indians in the skilled grades are mainly younger men who began working as apprentices during the last decade or so.

[1] Gardner, 1946, pp. 6–7.

A further distinction can be drawn between types and degrees of skill. The bulk of factory labourers tend the boilers, mills and pumps. Though their tasks can be graded in terms of function and skill, their work is in fact purely routine; the work of the workshop labourers is more varied, since each repair job presents a problem of diagnosis and requires an adaptation of techniques to a partly new situation. They are among the best paid workers in the factory. Fully qualified pan-boilers, who have undergone a long training, occupy a still higher place; senior pan-boilers are included among the Junior Staff and belong to the same income group as the foremen.

Differentiation in terms of skill is one of the most important contrasts between the field and the factory. So far as wages are concerned, the degree of skill is not important among field labourers; payment is made at a flat rate—so many cents per foot of drain dug or so many dollars per ton of cane cut. Where payment is made by the day or by the hour, the rate is the same for all. This does not mean that there is no such thing as a skilled shovel-man or a strong cane-cutter. But whether a man is skilled or not he is paid at a given rate.[1] The 'take home pay' differs from individual to individual, but this is the result of varying capacities for work, regularity of attendance, and 'obstacles' for which additional payment may be made.[2] In principle, all field labourers are evaluated as equals.

The 'take home pay' of factory labourers, on the other hand, depends on different rates of pay. A person who starts work in the factory is 'put' at a certain rate, i.e. at so many cents an hour, according to his grading by the factory manager on the advice of the overseer or foreman. Factory labour roles are thus evaluated individually. Two men may be employed as electricians but one may receive 26 cents an hour while the other receives 20. As a result factory workers, unlike field labourers, are conscious of individual differentiation and worth.

In consequence of the official recognition of grades of skill, avenues of upward occupational mobility are open to the factory labourer from apprentice up to runner[3] and foreman. In the field gang there is only one position a labourer can rise to, that of driver. In each gang there are at most two or three such posts, while the number of potential aspirants may amount to hundreds. Chances of promotion are so slender that most field labourers have given up any hope of it. The field labourer who starts work as a cane-cutter at a certain rate knows that twenty years later he will be paid at the same rate, even though he may be quite skilled at this occupation. The factory labourer starts work as an apprentice at, say 10 cents an hour but can reasonably expect, in course of time, to earn up to 30 cents an hour

[1] It does happen that when there is a shortage of work the overseer may select those whom he knows to be the more efficient workers. But this is regarded—by the labourers—as a breach of the norm and could lead to friction.

[2] See below, Chapter 4.

[3] An 'assistant foreman' who may be in charge of a shift.

and more. Consequently, compared to the field labourer, he is more concerned with his level of achievement and, like the clerks, is motivated by values of self-improvement.

Moreover, in contrast to the organization of field gangs, relationships in the factory are regulated in terms of authority and control. There is more careful observation of time-schedules, plans of work, and checks on levels of performance by foremen, overseers and time-keepers. In the field gang a driver intervenes only to prevent glaring inefficiency or breaches of discipline. There is, usually, little difference between two drains dug to the same specifications. Field labourers recognize this and resent any 'interference' by drivers who, therefore, confine themselves to maintaining the pace of work. But in the factory, job-cards and time-sheets enable foremen and overseers to keep a close check on levels of performance. Inefficient work is more obvious in the repair of an engine than in the digging of drains or the planting of cane tops. The grading of skills and rates of pay provide overseers and foremen with a very adequate mechanism for controlling the behaviour of factory labourers.

Relations between factory labourers reflect these conditions; the authority of one person over another is accepted. Thus the authority of the foreman is recognized as deriving from his greater skill and experience and is generally accepted. In the field gang the driver's authority is derived from his appointment by management solely on grounds of his loyalty and ability to discipline the gang—values which are not acceptable to the labourers who are apt to dub him a 'stooge'.

Further, factory labourers concede a certain authority to persons who do not have any specific office. When a group of labourers is assigned to a job the most skilled among them is placed in charge of the operation. But even though there may be no formal delegation of authority, the leadership of a higher-rated worker is accepted by his fellows and in return his technical advice is available at need. In the field there is no necessity for one labourer to call for the advice of another and, if it is offered, it may be resented as unjustified patronage.

However, even in the factory the situation is somewhat fluid and expectations of obedience are not so clear-cut that a definite pattern emerges. If one of the higher-rated men were to say, 'Where de pliers?', another worker is more likely to pick it up and bring it to him than if a lower-rated man were to say so. But there is no defined obligation to respond to his demand unless it is addressed to an assistant. The authority of a higher-rated man tends to be confirmed by general obedience to his wishes and repeated requests for his help from lower-rated men, though they have no obligation to do so.

OCCUPATION AND SOCIAL STATUS

Social stratification in the sugar plantations is based largely on a differential evaluation of occupational roles, expressed in the privileges, prestige, and honour accorded to each role. This status differentiation is officially recognized in that management formally classifies occupational roles into Senior Staff, Junior Staff, and Labourers, each of these categories constituting a status group. By and large the official classification corresponds closely to the classification of occupational roles into supervisory, clerical and labouring made on pages 29-30. Nevertheless there are a few instructive exceptions. The following chart correlates the occupational and official classifications:

	Supervisory	Clerical	Labouring
Senior Staff:	Manager	Accountant	
	Overseer		
	Engineer		
	Housing Officer		
	Chemist		
	Doctor		
Junior Staff:	Field clerk	Book-keeper	Pan-boiler
	Driver	Store-keeper	Distiller
	Foreman	Typist	
Labourers:			Electrician
			Tractor-operator
			Mechanic
			Carpenter
			Porter
			Cane-cutter
			Shovel-man
			Fork-man
			Weeder
			Dock worker
			Mule-boy
			Watchman
			Boiler attendant
			Mill-hand
			Punt baler

Status distinctions imply differential rights and duties in the organization of the plantation employees as a residential group. They determine social relations in many sectors of social action, govern expectations, and channel behaviour in recognizable patterns. It is therefore possible to speak of a mode of behaviour characteristic of each status group. The rest of this chapter will be devoted to a discussion of the general characteristics of these different modes of behaviour.

There are a score of Senior Staff households in Blairmont. Out of a sample of 379 of the 402 Indian households in Blairmont, 40 belonged to Junior Staff, 57 to skilled labourers and 276 to unskilled labourers. The rest were not plantation employees.

The Senior Staff

The chart shows that the coincidence between the occupational structure

CSGP D

and the status-group structure is not complete. Certain supervisory roles
—field clerks, drivers and foremen—do not belong to the Senior Staff. In
seeking a basis for an accurate definition of this status group one is tempted
to bring in an ethnic criterion, for the Senior Staff is to all intents and
purposes European. But this does not cover the whole group. Further,
although ethnic affiliation was an important qualification in the past, conditions are changing now and the 'Guianization' of at least some Senior
Staff positions is under way. The Senior Staff in Blairmont included one
Portuguese, one 'Mixed', one Eurasian and two Indians. The Senior Staff
in Port Mourant included two Portuguese, one Eurasian and one 'Mixed'.
The non-European proportions in these groups are between one-fifth and
a quarter.

The inclusion of two Indians in the Senior Staff can be explained on the
basis of Smith's view that the Indians in British Guiana occupy a marginal
position in the colour hierarchy. But the colour hierarchy, as he points out,
is not sufficient by itself to explain the Guianese system of social stratification. For instance, Indian field clerks who perform the same functions
as European overseers are graded as Junior Staff, but this cannot be explained solely by the low status of non-European ethnic affiliation. For a
very dark-skinned Negro in a neighbouring plantation belonged to the
Senior Staff there. Colour or ethnic affiliation is not, therefore, an invari-
able criterion of social status.[1]

Style of life is a more definitive criterion, for adherence to the style of
life associated with each status group is indispensable for membership in it.
There is considerable opposition from members of Senior Staffs to attempts
of the head office in Georgetown to promote drivers to the overseer
grade. It appears that the grounds for this opposition are not race or colour
but the inclusion in the communal life of the Senior Staff of persons whose
style of life is different and incompatible. The probability of this explanation is confirmed by the acceptance as status peers of non-European officials from the head office in Georgetown. The high occupational status of
these persons implies a familiarity with a similar style of life.

However, high occupational status alone is not sufficient evidence of
familiarity with a particular style of life. The behaviour of some non-
European members of the Senior Staff is instructive in this respect. An
Indian or Negro doctor may be accepted with few reservations, for he will
have been educated in England, possesses highly rated technical and social
skills and, as a member of the Guianese élite is, to some extent, 'to the
manner born'. A non-European Assistant Chemist, on the other hand,
probably started his career at a junior clerical level and has been promoted
after about twenty years' service to a position which entitles him to Senior
Staff privileges. He is probably not adept at the social skills of this style

[1] For a discussion of the function of race and colour in the social stratification
of Guianese society see Smith, 1956, pp. 191–203. Comparable West Indian
material is found in Braithwaite, 1953.

of life. Consequently he would tend to reduce personal contact with the rest of the Senior Staff to a minimum. A non-European who had been promoted from driver to overseer was noticeably timid and circumspect in the Senior Staff Club. He exhibited a completely different personality when visiting Junior Staff friends to eat curry and drink rum.

The style of life characteristic of the Senior Staff may be illustrated by a multitude of features but it will suffice to mention a few. One is 'European' food—bread, meat, vegetables, and a variety of imported foods such as bacon, ham, sausages, etc.—as distinct from the creole and Indian food of the labourers—rice, roti, curry, peas and 'ground provisions.' These last types of food are occasionally consumed by the Senior Staff but only as local specialities. Rum is drunk by all status groups but the Senior Staff sometimes drink whisky—a drink hardly ever consumed by labourers.

Clothing is another distinctive feature. The typical working clothes of a member of the Senior Staff are khaki or white shirts and short trousers, knee-length hose and a broad-brimmed hat. Apparently there was a time, in Blairmont, when only members of the Senior Staff were permitted to wear short trousers. That time has passed, and several labourers wear short trousers today, though without hose. The Senior Staff ride horses or mules when going into the field, but this method of transport is gradually being replaced by the motor bicycle, which is becoming a similar badge of high status. The status of the field clerk—which is intermediate between a driver and an overseer—is marked by the fact that he is the only non-member of the Senior Staff who has the 'right' to ride a mule into the field.

Membership in the Senior Staff is symbolized above all by the occupation of bungalows in the spacious Senior Staff Compound and by membership of the exclusive Senior Staff Club. The amenities of the Club include a bar, a billiard table, a swimming pool and the provision of novels and illustrated papers. Films are shown here and the wives of members meet for tea in the mornings. Every evening members gather to play games, drink, and chat.

Junior Staff

The Junior Staff is an intermediate group, though its lower line of demarcation is unclear. The official criterion, that all monthly paid employees fall into this category, lacks the sociological implications necessary to define a status group. All clerks belong to it by virtue of their education and the social prestige attaching to white collar jobs. Drivers and foremen belong to it because their supervisory role supports their claim to a status higher than that of the labourers. The Chief Electrician (who is also a foreman) and the senior pan-boilers belong to it, but not other electricians and pan-boilers. Although it takes as long to acquire the skills of a good electrician or a good pan-boiler as those of a clerk, a low evaluation of manual labour places them in an inferior position. The status of technical skills in a society with an under-developed economy appears still undecided. Yet the presence of a factory in the midst of the community, and the group of skilled technicians attached to it present a constant challenge to the older social status system in which drivers and clerks alone could reach a social status above that of the labourer.

In so far as a characteristic style of life can be attributed to the Junior Staff, it is that of clerks rather than drivers and foremen. There is an important difference in their backgrounds. The drivers and foremen began work as labourers. Normally it would have taken them about twenty years to reach their present position. During this period they would have been completely adapted to the labourer's style of life. Culturally, there is much more in common between a driver and a labourer than between a clerk and a labourer.

Most clerks have had three to four years' schooling in a secondary school in town after leaving the local primary school. A few of them have studied for the Cambridge Senior and the G.C.E. examinations. This long period of education implies that their parents could afford to send their children to secondary schools. Thus clerks tend to come from the more prosperous families. A few are the sons of drivers and represent a second generation which has risen above the status of labourer.

As a result of their experience of secondary school education clerks are more ready to adopt Guianese middle-status values than labourers are. Self-improvement and an absorbing interest in acquiring canons of etiquette and propriety are striking features of their group ideology.[1] They emphasize their superior status by frequently commenting on the lack of education and 'respectability' among the labourers. Even when a clerk lives with his labourer parents he presents a clear example of 'anticipatory socialization'.[2]

The Junior Staff Club is the hallmark of membership in this status group. The facilities available here are a modest reflection of those available at the Senior Staff Club—a bar, easy chairs, magazines, etc. Table-tennis replaces billiards and there is no swimming pool. The principal ceremony is the annual Christmas dance to which the Senior Staff is invited but not the labourers. Most of the former do not attend, but the latter stand outside in great numbers. Still, the Administrative Manager and a few other senior personnel, accompanied by their wives, pay a brief token visit. Members of the Junior Staff and visiting Senior Staff personnel make several long speeches to each other across the dance floor. The Manager formally opens proceedings by asking one of the typists for a dance, and an intrepid clerk reciprocates by inviting the manager's wife. The Senior Staff guests leave early, while the dance continues watched by a crowd of youths peering in from outside. This is almost the only contact between the Senior and Junior Staffs outside working hours.

[1] A framed copy of Kipling's poem 'If' is a favourite adornment in the homes of clerks.
[2] Merton, 1958, pp. 265–8. The 'reference group' of this socialization is the middle-status group of Guianese society.

The only dietary differences between Junior Staff and labourers are those resulting from the higher incomes of the former. The clothes of clerks are generally cleaner than those of labourers. They wear shoes and ties; jackets are worn on formal occasions. The working dress of drivers stands out like a uniform—khaki trousers and shirt and a walking stick or umbrella. They and the overseers also wear a slouch hat which is an important badge of status.

Drivers and labourers speak the same low-status dialect of English, known as *taki-taki*. But clerks speak the prestige-endowing 'high English', a distinguishing feature of which is the use of many decorous circumlocutions. Within the Junior Staff group there are several differences in patterns of behaviour between the clerks and the drivers. In these matters drivers warily follow in the footsteps of the clerks, though a few of them who are still in their thirties may participate more actively by helping to organize sports and dances, and serving on the club committee.

Clerks emphasize distinctions between themselves and the labourers and attempt to enforce social restrictions whenever possible. In the office, seated behind a desk, a clerk can keep a labourer standing in front of him, address him brusquely, and accentuate his status superiority in a variety of other ways. ('Him tink he ah manager, but him ah who?' an indignant labourer once shouted, pointing an accusing finger at a clerk.) The houses of clerks are not separated from those of the labourers, but they maintain only sporadic contact with low-status neighbours. One of them, for example, stated that he did not wish to associate with such people because they were untrustworthy, troublesome, and given to drinking and swearing. He visited them as rarely as possible and sought the company of his fellow clerks who lived in other settlements. Few clerks are present at informal gatherings such as *pujas*, 'cook-nights', and conversational groups in cake-shops. But they attend major ceremonies such as weddings and wakes.

Yet status differentiation between Junior Staff and labourers is not complete. A clerk is bound by ties of kinship, marriage, religious affiliation, and the exigencies of living in densely populated neighbourhoods—particularly if he lives with his labourer parents. It makes their claim to a distinct and superior status a matter of some doubt.

A distinctive Junior Staff style of life is still in process of crystallization; among clerks, but not among drivers, it is possible to trace the emergence of distinctive patterns. The labourers accord the Junior Staff a certain superiority and prestige but at the same time criticize them for their uppishness, their claims to gentility, and their 'betrayal' of their origins— 'Dem ah forget dem ah Indian.' The Junior Staff, on the other hand, talk of the lack of education, the uncouth manners and the stupidity of the labourers.

Skilled and Unskilled Labourers

Labourers form the lowest status group and their skills are rated much lower than those of the Senior and Junior Staff. Evaluations of skill within the group of labourers, however, lead to a distinction between skilled and unskilled labourers. A valued skill, relatively high and regular wages, and the ability to 'hold down a work' gives the skilled labourer a certain prestige. There is much competition for work in the factory and jobs as operators of tractors and drag-lines. The ambition of many young field labourers is to 'get a mechanic work'. Skilled labourers compete for prestige with the Junior Staff, and challenge the assertion of superiority by the clerks. On the other hand there is close contact between skilled and unskilled labourers, and the distinctions between them should not be pressed too far for these are hardly ever formalized or made explicit.

Nevertheless, in discussing the social status of the labourers the several ties between them and the Junior Staff should be borne in mind; labourers do not constitute distinct status groups in all social situations. In Blairmont there is more intermingling between the two groups than in Port Mourant, where the cleavage is more pronounced because there is a wider circle of school-teachers, shop-assistants and clerks in Rosehall with whom the Junior Staff of the plantation can associate, so that its members are less dependent on the labourers. Further, in both plantations drivers maintain close contact with the labourers and form another link between the two groups.

Differences in marriage customs, marital stability, family structure, religion, education, and standards of living help to distinguish the styles of life characteristic of the two groups. It should be noted, however, that these distinctive patterns are not exclusive to either group. The same traits are found in both but in varying proportions. No one of these determines an individual's social status; it is the cluster of traits that demarcates the status groups and places individual persons. In the following paragraphs I shall briefly indicate the bases on which the Junior Staff and the labourers can be distinguished.

Most plantation Indians marry according to Hindu or Muslim customary rites, but such marriages are not legally valid unless registered with the Immigration Department or, since 1957, with a licensed marriage officer who may be a Hindu or Muslim priest. The first marriage is usually of the customary type without legal registration. If this proves stable it is legalized, usually after six to ten years. If the marriage breaks up before that, the partners enter into common-law (consensual) unions which are legalized if they prove to be stable. It is therefore useful to distinguish four types of marriage: customary, customary and legal, legal only, and common-law.

In Blairmont nearly two-thirds of the married men are living in non-legal marriages, in Port Mourant only about a fifth. The difference is largely due to the fact that in Port Mourant most families own the house they live in, and since legal marriage safeguards the wife's rights of inheritance, the ownership of property is one incentive to legalize a marriage.

Middle-status group ideals of respectability are another. According to the central standards of the society, a non-legal marriage is not respectable; this is especially true of common-law marriages. The marriages established by Indian customary rites are accorded a certain validity for, though legal marriage with a church wedding is a core institution, Indian customary rites are a permitted alternative.[1]

Customary marriages are found in all status groups, but common-law marriages are not found among clerks in either Blairmont or Port Mourant. The majority of the Junior Staff in Blairmont and all in Port Mourant are legally married. On the other hand most of the common-law marriages in Blairmont (52 out of 58) and all those in Port Mourant are found among unskilled labourers. The skilled labourers occupy an intermediate position. I have shown elsewhere that marriage is more stable among the Junior Staff than among the unskilled labourers and have attributed this to the stronger authority of the husband/father in higher-status group families as well as to an ethical aversion to separation and non-legal marriage.[2]

Hindus, Muslims and Christians are found in all status groups; however, most of the Christians are found among the Junior Staff among whom, too, there are significantly larger proportions of reformists (Arya Samaj and Ahmediya). The more rational and modernized theologies of the reformist movements fit in better with the more creolized culture of the Junior Staff. The unskilled labourers are predominantly orthodox believers.

The style of life distinctive of the Junior Staff is that of Guianese 'petit bourgeois' status groups which is a variant of 'European culture'. The Indian immigrants were absorbed into creole society at the lowest status level. Upward mobility was achieved through (a) familiarization with the customs and values of the wider society and a corresponding decrease in adherence to 'coolie custom', and (b) economic betterment. The first avenues lie through education.[3] Indeed it is at school that Indians first acquire the status characteristics of learning to speak 'high English', and middle-status canons of propriety.

Experience of school, measured in terms of educational attainment, is significantly different for each of the status groups. Nearly half of the clerks in Blairmont and nearly two-thirds of those in Port Mourant have been to secondary school. Less than one percent of the unskilled labourers in the two plantations have done so. All the clerks in Blairmont and Port Mourant have studied up to the 5th Standard, while only about a fifth of the unskilled labourers have done so. Among the unskilled labourers about a fifth in Blairmont and a quarter in Port Mourant have had no schooling at all. The skilled labourers occupy an intermediate position.

---

[1] Smith and Jayawardena, 1959.   [2] Jayawardena, 1960 and 1962.

[3] Smith, 1956, points out that among Negroes too one of the functions of the school was 'indoctrinating the pupils with the values of the total social system and teaching them its culture', p. 135. Stratification in a Negro village 'is largely in terms of cultural differences combined with occupational status', p. 206.

With less than four years' schooling, as is usual among unskilled labourers, an individual has little control over the techniques and skills that ensure high status and power both in the local community and in the wider society. English is the language of the Administration and the medium of communication in the society as a whole. To the extent that an unskilled labourer is not competent in the language (in its standard form) he is cut off from the sources of information and power. Whether he is bargaining for better conditions, or computing wages, or asserting his rights, he is at a disadvantage and dependent on others. As an individual an unskilled labourer is an under-privileged person. His power in the social system is slight and his ability to protect himself is limited.

Besides language and education, differences between the groups appear in their standards of living, for example in dress, diet and household furnishing. A 'typical' labourer is dressed in khaki or white shirt and trousers. He does not usually wear shoes except on special occasions; skilled labourers usually wear canvas shoes and are relatively better dressed. The nature of their work, to some extent, dictates the labourers' dress, but it tends to become habitual and almost a mark of identity.

The type of food eaten by the local group as a whole is referred to, in the context of Guianese culture, as 'Indian'; but in fact the diet of all groups comprises the same range of foods, and the differences between groups appear in the frequency with which the more expensive items, such as meat, fish, and milk, are bought. Most families keep fowls, but the poorer families prefer to sell the birds and eggs rather than eat them.

Usually there is no lack of rice. Management provides each labourer who has worked for a certain time with half an acre for planting rice, and the harvest from this plot supplies the needs of the average family for more than half the year. The security that an adequate stock of rice provides invests it with an almost symbolic importance, especially among unskilled labourers, whose earnings are meagre and irregular, because even when income has dwindled to nothing the household can still subsist on its rice, with an occasional fish caught in the river or leaves picked in the bush. During periods of unemployment unskilled labourers live largely on such a diet.

The Junior Staff is not provided with rice fields. Some buy their rice and others rent fields in the village. The fact that clerks can still work in the rice fields without loss of prestige confirms the impression that status differences in behaviour have not yet crystallized. However, the practice of using hired labour is becoming increasingly common.

Plenitude and variety of food throughout the year is a status attribute, for it is recognized that families which have to search for food during a part of the year cannot meet as real social equals families which do not. 'Ah we home get plenty fu eat' and 'Dem ah beggar; dem nah get money fu eat' are statements about prestige.

A similar difference is reflected in household furniture and other effects, that is to say in the frequency with which such items as dressing-tables, wardrobes, chairs, sewing machines, pressure lanterns, radios, and bicycles are found in the households of Junior Staff and labourers.

Income

Social status can be broadly correlated with income. The following table attempts to do this for Blairmont. Not all the employees are included because, in the pay-lists, names are not classified by type of occupation, and many labourers are known on the plantation by names different from those used outside.[1] The figures relate only to those whose identities could be established. No female workers have been included.

The first column gives the number of persons in each occupational category from whose wages these figures were extracted. The highest, lowest and average wages are annual totals. 'Days Available' refers to the average number of days on which work was available during the year for each occupational category, and 'Days Worked' refers to the average number of days on which these labourers were present at work. These items do not apply to Junior Staff for whom attendance is compulsory because they are paid monthly.

TABLE 5

Income and Occupational Status[2]

	Number	Highest wage p.a.	Lowest wage p.a.	Average wage p.a.	Days available	Days worked
Junior Staff						
Clerks	21	$2,400.00	$660.00	$1,083.96	—	—
Drivers	19	1,440.00	780.00	1,036.56	—	—
Skilled Labourers						
Factory	22	1,474.81	636.34	951.20	286	280
Field	14	1,552.59	653.68	873.86	260	258
Unskilled Labourers						
Cane-cutters	44	1,204.56	121.84	694.46	215	162
Cane Transport	21	1,097.81	119.62	464.00	188	157
Watchmen and Rangers	17	916.24	138.98	537.70	268	234
Fork- and Shovel-men	56	866.48	46.38	388.96	173	126
Weeders and Manurers	13	798.21	59.35	374.30	230	182

One important point that emerges from these figures is that the main

[1] People are often given names when they first start work by the overseer or driver. The 'pay-list name' bears no relation to the 'born name'.
[2] I am greatly indebted to Mr Bharatlal of the Blairmont Office who helped me to collect these figures.

disparity lies between the Junior Staff and the skilled labourers on the one hand and the unskilled labourers on the other. So far as the Junior Staff and the skilled labourers are concerned, it is clear that a good skilled labourer can earn as much as, if not more than, a clerk or a driver although, on an average, a member of the Junior Staff may be expected to earn more. Similarly, some unskilled labourers, e.g. a cane-cutter, can also earn as much as some clerks, drivers, and skilled labourers. But he cannot keep up this level for his income begins to diminish as his strength begins to wane and sooner or later he will end as a shovel-man or a watchman. Yet the table bears out the fact that, in so far as it is correlated with social status, income distribution is a continuum, with no sharp breaks between one group and another. Given the same amount of effort, a member of the Junior Staff, on an average, earns more than a skilled labourer, and the latter more than an unskilled labourer.

I make the qualification 'effort' advisedly, for there is an interesting difference in attendance at work between skilled and unskilled labourers. The following table presents the average figures of days worked and days available for the two groups.

TABLE 6

Attendance at Work, Blairmont 1957

	Number	Average no. of days available	Average no. of days worked	Percentage
Skilled Labourers	36	276	272	98·5
Unskilled Labourers	151	203	158	77·7

Since unskilled labourers are poorer than skilled labourers, if the former were motivated entirely by economic aims, one would expect them to turn up for work whenever it was available. But this is not so. The unskilled labourers worked 77·7 per cent of the average number of days available while the skilled labourers worked 98·5 per cent.

Thus the skilled labourer who is better paid works harder than the unskilled labourer who is worse paid. The explanation for this is complex. One reason is the unpredictable way in which work is made available for the unskilled labourer. He seldom gets a week's notice of when work is available, and consequently finds it difficult to plan his time; thus, other commitments often clash with his work. The only activity, however, which poses a serious problem of choice is work in the rice fields. But the rice harvest does not usually coincide with the cane harvest and much of the rice work can be so arranged that it does not clash with the 'available' days. Moreover, the unskilled labourer does not have more than an average of four days' work a week. It is therefore not difficult to avoid a clash of claims.

The discussion of absenteeism and attitudes to work in a study of a Yorkshire coal-mining community[1] contains some useful suggestions. The

[1] Dennis, Henriques, and Slaughter, 1956.

authors point out that the miners regard work as an unfortunate necessity. After the good wage of a hard week's work a miner is prepared to 'buy his leisure' by taking a day or two off during the following week. Similarly, in the plantation there is a strong tradition of 'de estate punish ah we coolie people', the punishment being labour. To the unskilled labourer, earning a living by the sweat of his brow is a misfortune he is born to ('God work') and not a duty. The arduousness of much of the work confirms this attitude. The Venn Commission Report provides figures which show that cane-cutters' attendance drops just before and just after the week-end and reaches a maximum at mid-week.[1] Dennis, Henriques, and Slaughter report similarly on miners.

In contrast, many skilled labourers take great pride in their skill and are extremely conscientious. Many of them work extra days overtime. Visitors and friends are importuned to watch them operate machines. Unskilled labourers would interpret a desire to watch them work as a gesture of sympathy. Several objected to being photographed at work because they would 'look ugly'.

The unskilled labourers' attitude to work is closely associated with a kind of hedonism and is to be contrasted with the element of the 'Protestant ethic' in the attitude of skilled labourers. This same feature has been noted by Dennis, Henriques and Slaughter, who describe it as 'frivolousness', defining frivolous as 'giving no thought for the morrow'.[2] They point out that it is an aspect of the deep feeling of insecurity created by fluctuating wages and uncertain employment. The same sense of insecurity is apparent in many idiomatic expressions commonly used by plantation labourers: a promise is often prefaced with the condition 'God willing', and an appointment or plan for the future is qualified by the expression 'if me still alive'.

A notable example of this hedonism is the enormous consumption of rum. Members of the lower-status groups drink much more heavily than those of the higher groups, who spend a relatively larger portion of their income on improving their standard of living and making provision for their children's education and their own old age. Several clerks, drivers and skilled labourers have taken out insurance policies. Many indicate with pride their dedication to 'improving meself', in contrast to the lower-status spendthrifts who are like 'kiskides on cow-back' (gadflies) and 'drink dey money out'. Many unskilled labourers whose families are in desperate need of money spend their bonuses and 'holiday with pay' lump sums on treating their friends to rum and chicken curry. Although a number of cane-cutters earn $700.00 and more, they as well as poorer labourers experience great hardship during the lean period. In the harvest season some money is saved and deposited in the post office savings bank or invested in jewellery for the wife. But these savings are withdrawn during the non-earning weeks, and the wife's jewellery is carried to and fro

[1] *Report*, 1949, p. 73. [2] op. cit., pp. 130-1.

between the pawnshop and the home. Dennis, Henriques and Slaughter, discussing a similar situation in Ashton, relate the disproportionate expenditure on luxuries to insecurity of employment and fluctuating income:

> There is a temporary sense of loss attendant upon the deprival of even the most trivial possession which is avoided if possible. . . . By keeping his standard of living low in relation to necessities, the miner avoids that permanent sense of loss suffered by decayed gentlemen and gentlewomen.[1]

This statement is equally applicable to unskilled plantation workers.

Another heavy item of expenditure is hospitality. In rural British Guiana there are no large-scale amusement businesses to attract the money of those ready to spend it. Except for the local cinema, which may be several miles away, and an occasional brothel in town, there are no organized institutions for entertainment. The labourer who has money to spend uses it to entertain friends.

Egalitarian Norms

High expenditure on conviviality has the important function of helping to maintain the solidarity of the group. The formal structure of labour relations emphasizes the independence of each labourer, but there is an 'informal structure' which maintains group cohesion. The organizing principle here is the equality of social status and prestige among all labourers expressed in the notion of *mati*.[2]

The term is used in a variety of contexts and with many shades of meaning. At the core of its meaning is the tie between persons associated at work. The whole gang, or all the labourers of the plantation, or the plantation labourers of Demerara as well, can be included, depending on the context. The association is recognized as close-knit and *mati* sometimes means one of a couple (e.g. a marriage may be described as 'they took *mati*'). A degree of amity is also implied. For instance, a man who rudely snubbed another was reprimanded with, 'Man, wha make you shit-up *mati* so?' To describe two persons fighting as 'they beat *mati*' is either an implicit criticism of deviation from a norm or an indication that the fight was a friendly one.

There are degrees of *mati*, and the more the sentiment is felt the stronger the friendship. The ideal is realized when, during periods of scarce employment, those who get work one day stay away on the next 'to give *mati* a chance'. This is not often done but when it is, public acclaim is demanded. Here the key connotation is the bond in equality presumed to exist between

---

[1] op. cit., p. 139.

[2] It is probable that the word is derived from the English word 'mate'. It is in common use both among Indians and Negroes, and was presumably borrowed by the former from the latter. Herskovits reports its use among the Negroes of Surinam in the sense of a close friendship. However, in Surinam it is also used in the special sense of a homosexual relationship which I have not heard in British Guiana. Herskovits, 1936.

the two parties. They do the same type of work, they both have families to feed, they face the same difficulties, they are equally endowed so that differences in fortune are due to luck rather than any 'superiority'; therefore one person should share his good fortune with his fellow. So he stays at home and gives his neighbour a chance to earn a day's wage. Mutual consideration is the proper mode of behaviour between *mati*.

Mati implies persons of equal social status and power. A labourer never refers to a manager as his *mati*, but he may explain a manager's support of an overseer's decision as 'they supporting *mati*'. In some contexts members of the Junior Staff are included in the relationship. This is possible because equality and mutuality of interests between the two groups are recognized in some sectors such as participation in Indian culture. *Mati*, then, may be defined as a relationship between persons of relatively equal social status which should be characterized by amity, respect, and consideration for the interests and prestige of each. However, it is important to remember that it is a very flexible term which can be used in a variety of relationships and situations.

Several conditions of labour support the sentiments of *mati*, especially among unskilled labourers, among whom it provides a pattern of behaviour to counteract the individualism of the formal structure. Each shovel-man digs his own drain, each fork-man plants his own bed, and each pair of cane-cutters load one punt. They are paid on the basis of 'each according to his work'. But, if the soil is hard for one shovel-man it is hard for others working in that part of the field. If the cane is not well burnt or the ground sodden all cane-cutters find reaping difficult. One labourer may have greater skill or strength than another and earn more, but both work under the same conditions and are paid at the same rate. What one deserves, all deserve; all are *mati*.

The recognition of this bond is crucial in disputes with management. I shall discuss these in the following chapter; it will suffice to point out here that, in bargaining over the rate to be paid for the job, it is advantageous for the labourers to have no dissidents in their ranks. If a minority of shovel-men maintain that the soil is 'normal' and not hard, or if a minority of cane-cutters are satisfied with the state of the cane, the case for higher rates for the group as a whole is undermined. Furthermore, the threat to strike is ineffective if there is no unity. The sentiment of *mati* with its connotations of equality and mutual consideration is influential in creating this unity.

Inter-gang mobility is also conducive to the maintenance of *mati*. It prevents the gang from becoming a closed group, for the resultant fluidity in the composition of gangs inhibits the formation of occupational subgroups with sectional interests. Most unskilled labourers have worked in several branches of field labour, and this varied experience gives each a wide range of contacts and increases his number of face-to-face relationships. Usually he has worked in a gang with almost every other fellow resident at some time or other and has at least a nodding acquaintance with everyone else in the community. Everyone is or should be *mati*.

The solidarity thus engendered can be quite strong. In one instance a labourer of the Cane Transport gang was suspended for negligence. The first reaction of a group of unskilled labourers, none of them cane-cutters, was to condemn the 'injustice' of the manager's decision. But soon arguments were forthcoming to the effect that the negligence of the labourer concerned had delayed the supply of empty punts to the field, causing the cane-cutters some inconvenience and financial loss. This changed the attitude of the group to one of censure of the man who, by his indifference, caused his *mati* a loss. Because of his varied experience each labourer can understand the grievances of his fellows, even though he is not currently employed in the same type of work. The sentiment of *mati* unites all occupational categories of the field. One person's cause can become everyone's cause.

To a limited extent the sentiment of *mati* unites the unskilled field labourers with the skilled factory labourers. Several factory labourers have worked a few years in the field and therefore have a sympathetic understanding of the problems of the field labourers. Still, it should be noted that skilled labourers are not as ready to see relations between themselves or between themselves and unskilled labourers as governed by the norms of *mati*. They may do the same work, they may even co-operate on the same job, but they are paid at different rates. Again, there is little horizontal occupational mobility in the factory, where a skilled trade is the specialization of a lifetime. Consequently the recognition of bonds of *mati* among skilled labourers is modified by the awareness of differences in individual achievement and skill. But there are other sectors of the social system in which the relationship of *mati* can be and is established, such as the structure of authority and labour-management relations, kinship and neighbourhood, and participation in a variety of ceremonies. Factory labourers have made common cause with field labourers in many strikes.

One of the ways in which the tie of *mati* is affirmed is conviviality, especially drinking together, which signifies social equality. Normally, to refuse an invitation to drink is regarded as a repudiation of this equality. In plantations drinking has a strong ritual element in that it 'serves to express the individual's status as a social person in the structural system in which he finds himself for the time being'.[1] Certain categories of persons may be exempted from accepting invitations, but on clearly defined grounds, for instance, persons intent on doing 'priest-work' or 'leading de sadhu life'; but in general the person who refuses a drink should be able to validate his refusal by his superior social status as overseer, driver or clerk.

Drinking sessions are characterized by a highly formalized series of actions. They may almost be described as 'communions' which reaffirm

[1] Leach, 1954, pp. 10–16.

the bonds of the group. The company sits around a table on which bottles of rum[1] as well as soft drinks and a jug of water are placed. Each person has a 'snap glass'[2] before him, The host opens the bottle by first striking its base vigorously with his palm, an action which, it is said, facilitates the opening of the vacuum-sealed bottle. It is customary to pour out the first drops on the floor 'for the spirits'. Each member of the company then washes out his glass with water from the jug. This is sometimes done out of sheer habit, even when the glasses appear perfectly clean. One might interpret this as a 'survival' of caste practices were it not that Negroes do the same. Each drinker fills his little glass and swallows the neat rum in one gulp. Then the 'chaser', either water or the soft drink, is poured out and similarly gulped down. All raise the full glass and lower the empty one together. A person drinking at his own pace is rare, and slackers are urged to keep up with the rest of the company. The glasses are then washed for the next round, especially if a soft drink was used as a chaser. The rounds follow each other regularly, interspersed with intervals of conversation and gossip, until the stock of liquor is finished. I have seldom seen a bottle put away after a few drinks, and by custom every opened bottle is emptied.

Normally these gatherings are composed of males only. Females, such as the wife of the host, come in occasionally with snacks and food or are seated some distance away. Sometimes the wives of those present gather in the kitchen. I was told that women also assemble behind closed doors for all-female drinking sessions, but my impression is that these are extremely infrequent and not as prevalent as many men assert, for husbands normally disapprove of their wives drinking.

The ceremonial character of drinking is emphasized by the fact that very few drink alone. Despite the enormous quantity of liquor consumed there are not more than two or three who can be described as alcoholics in the generally accepted sense of the term.[3] In the local dialect the term for an alcoholic, 'rum-sucker', is an extremely offensive epithet never applied to social drinkers however hard they may drink. The solitary drinkers are men who have dropped out of the social circle through lack of means or for some other reason. In Blairmont they tended to drink 'bush rum'[4] or surgical spirit, both of which reduce the drinker's prestige. The situation is different in Port Mourant where the manufacture of bush rum flourishes. It is sold for as little as 50 cents a bottle and is a more socially permitted

---

[1] Popular brands such as 'Old Grog' (manufactured in Blairmont) and 'Russian Bear' used to cost $2.00 (8s. 4d.) per bottle. Cheaper brands can be bought at rum shops which blend their own rum.

[2] A small glass with a capacity equal to a bar measure.

[3] Keller, 1958, defines alcoholism as 'a chronic behavioural disorder manifested by repeated drinking of alcoholic beverages in excess of the dietary and social uses of the community'. See also Bacon, 1958.

[4] The local 'moonshine', brewed with molasses and ammonia, and then distilled. The first bottle out of the barrel is quite palatable. Subsequent bottles tend to be mixed with sediment.

drink. The legal penalties for its manufacture, consumption, or possession are draconian; nevertheless, it is consumed in some haven secluded from the police. Its popularity in Port Mourant is a recent phenomenon, probably due to under-employment since the factory closed down. The social importance of drinking created the need for a type of liquor within reach of the average diminished purse. Increased poverty did not reduce consumption.

Even a casual observer cannot fail to be struck by the lucrativeness of the liquor trade. The population of Blairmont is served by its own rum shop, by three just outside the plantation and a fourth about half a mile away. There are means of buying rum from shops after closing hours. Several stores without licenses sell rum under the counter and there are, in addition, enterprising individuals in each settlement-area who buy cases of rum at wholesale rates and sell them privately in their homes. The same is true of Port Mourant.

Drinking is only one of several ways in which sentiments of *mati* are expressed through conviviality. An element of conviviality enters into all traditional ceremonies associated with holy days, prayer meetings, marriages and funerals.

Conviviality maintains the bonds of *mati* indirectly by siphoning off wealth in excess of that required to maintain a minimum standard of living. Social equality is bound up with living at a similar standard, but differences in skill, strength, capacity to work and a variety of other factors result in unequal incomes and opportunities. Income in excess of the common level of requirements could be used for 'capital improvements', in raising living standards, saving and investment, acquiring prestige goods, etc., and so for asserting superior social status. But a high expenditure on conviviality prevents this potential cleavage within the relatively homogeneous group. Great esteem is attached to liberality[1] and parsimony is disapproved of. Low-status labourers in particular criticize more abstemious upwardly mobile persons on this score. The emphasis on spending thus performs a double function—reaffirming the bonds of *mati* and inhibiting status differentiation.

[1] For a description of conspicuous consumption in traditional weddings, see Smith and Jayawardena, 1958.

4

The Basis of Social Conflict

THE social system of the plantation community, as presented so far, is largely a static model. In its more dynamic aspect, as social process distinguished from social structure, it reveals a widespread incidence of conflict. The term 'conflict' is used here in accordance with Weber's definition:

A social relationship will be referred to as 'conflict' in so far as action within it is oriented intentionally to carrying out the actor's own will against the resistance of the other party or parties.[1]

By this definition, conflict is a mode of interaction between two or more persons in which the parties concerned attempt to control each other's behaviour. Conflict is thus a result of the exercise of power by persons or groups in situations in which social action is guided by mutually incompatible interests.[2]

The potentiality of conflict is an essential corollary of social structure. Differentiation into sub-groups implies differences of interests between them. Such differences do not necessarily result in conflict, but the integration of separate groups in a wider structure can lead to competition for status, power, and resources. The closer the integration the more will competing interests jostle with each other.

Incompatibility of interests may also arise from a person's membership in different kinds of sub-groups, e.g. kinship, religious, and social status groups, for behaviour in accordance with the norms of one group may be incompatible with behaviour in accordance with the norms of another. The degree to which such incompatibility of roles is tolerated depends on the degree of social cohesion. In a social structure in which roles are closely linked, incompatibility can be more effectively regulated than in a structure where roles are markedly differentiated and widely dispersed.

Conflicts occur at all levels of the structure of the plantation community —at the level of the community as a whole, at the level of its sub-groups and at the level of individual persons. This study deals mainly with

---

[1] Weber, 1947, p. 132.
[2] Bernard, 1957b, states, 'Conflict arises when there are incompatible or mutually exclusive goals or aims or values, espoused by human beings' (p. 38). I use the term 'interests' to cover 'goals, aims and values'.

inter-personal conflict. However, this topic cannot be studied in isolation from conflict occurring at other levels for, like the various parts of the social structure, conflicts are systematically interrelated. In this chapter I shall discuss the general pattern of conflict in the social system of the plantation and inter-personal conflicts in relation to it.

The demarcation of the local community in terms of sugar plantation, working class, and Indian, indicates some of the lines of cleavage across which conflicts involving the group as a whole can occur. As a group of labourers, plantation residents come into conflict with other classes for more effective representation in the legislature, for a greater share in the distribution of wealth, for social privileges, and for maintaining their own patterns of behaviour. One form of conflict at this level, which is of central importance in this study, is that with employers over wages and working conditions.

Ethnic differentiation is another line of cleavage across which conflict can occur. As Indians, the group is concerned with maintaining Indian culture and resisting wholesale creolization. The recognition of cultural differences creates stereotypes about the nature and actions of the 'coolie' and the 'blackman'. Ethnic conflict occurs in terms of criticism, ridicule, and invidious comparison of these stereotypes. No one disputes with another simply because the latter is a Negro, nor are there disputes between the local groups of Indians and Negroes in the plantation. The only 'racial' dispute that I observed arose over a Negro's remark that Indians were thin undersized weaklings. This view was supported by some Negroes and some Indians, and opposed by others. They decided to resolve the controversy by a fight between chosen champions, and members of each ethnic group backed the group's representative regardless of their opinions in the preceding argument. The contest was terminated by a policeman who arrested both champions for disorderly behaviour, but each side claimed the victory and declared that the opposing champion did not fight clean.

Another basis of conflict is the system of social stratification. The recognition of differences takes the form of hostile criticism. The Junior Staff considers the labourers to be uneducated and uncouth and the labourers consider them to be conceited and snobbish. The controversy implicit in these criticisms relates not to their existence as distinct status groups, but to the prestige each is willing to accord to the other.

Conflict in the kinship system is the result of the formation of nuclear families with competing interests. The close integration of a person's family of orientation with his family of procreation through common residence leads to conflict over the control of the services of husband and wife. The separation of resources is a commonly recognized method of reducing conflict of interests. The competing rights of affinally related groups to control the marriage they jointly sponsored is another source of disputes. The extent to which such disputes rupture relations depends on the extent to which marriages are legalized and affinal groups participate in communal activity. Within the nuclear family there is latent conflict between husband and wife for control over household resources.[1] The relative lack of common interests among adults of the same family, which is due to a general absence of productive property, makes inter-generation and sibling conflict infrequent. When such conflicts do occur the situation is one in which there is a common interest such as the conduct of a marriage or a funeral. Absence of interests is even more marked between collaterals and consequently disputes between them arising out of kinship obligations are extremely rare.

In religious activities both Hindus and Muslims take pains to avoid clashes of interests, and inter-group conflict is usually averted by an over-riding loyalty to the Indian group. Yet occasionally disputes do occur especially when one side breaks the tacit no-conversion agreement. Disputes between orthodox and reform groups are more unrestrained, and the sometimes bitter hostility between these groups bears out Simmel's proposition that the closer the similarity the more intense the conflict.[2] The orthodox groups have tried hard to keep the reformists out of the plantations and until recently succeeded in doing so. The theological differences between them are kept alive by a continuous indecisive controversy. Within each of these groups there is further conflict between cliques formed on various issues such as election to committees, appointment of priests, and the spending of funds.

The structure of the plantation community thus consists of a number of groups with different and opposed interests, working sometimes in co-operation and sometimes in conflict. The conflicts pertain to different sectors of social activity and the personnel of the groups which meet in the resultant disputes is never the same. Persons who oppose each other over the conduct of a marriage are not necessarily the same individuals who oppose each other for control of the church. Religious antagonisms cut across status distinctions which, in turn, straddle ethnic differences. The social structure of the plantation can be described in Gluckman's terms as a 'division of society into a series of opposed groups with cross-cutting membership'.[3]

Cross-cutting membership in a variety of opposed groups makes allies of persons who, in other contexts, are enemies and *vice versa*. Social status antagonism may unite persons who belong to different ethnic, kinship and religious groups, or it may draw a line of cleavage between persons who are otherwise allied. When one religious faction appeals to management to exercise sanctions against another, class antagonism is dominated, in that context, by religious antagonism. A multiplicity of intersecting ties, as Gluckman has noted,[4] promotes social cohesion. Persons opposed to each other in one situation of conflict are prevented from breaking away entirely,

---

[1] Jayawardena, 1960 and 1962.
[2] Simmel, 1955, pp. 47–8. See also Coser, 1956, pp. 67–72.
[3] Gluckman, 1954a, p. 67.   [4] ibid. See also Gluckman, 1955b.

or eliminating each other, by being anchored in alliance in another situation of conflict. The model of a social system which emerges from this analysis is one in which the opposition between the parts maintains the cohesion and order of the whole. A balanced opposition creates a stalemate between conflicting groups. One may expect, then, that such a system will remain stable for relatively long periods of time.

Yet, so far as the plantations are concerned, this model does not entirely fit the facts. For the internal balance of the system is continually broken up and remoulded by external forces such as government decisions, political developments, and the market. Government policy to develop trade unions can change the nature of conflict between management and labour by localizing disputes. It can also create new groupings among the labourers which compete for the control of the union. A deterioration in ethnic group relations fostered, for instance, by politicians at the national level, can emphasize ethnic distinctions in the plantation and correspondingly weaken social status distinctions, labour-management hostility and religious faction rivalry. A balanced opposition making for social cohesion and stability is to be found, if at all, only at the level of the total society. The only more or less permanent element of stability in the history of the plantations has been their organization for the production of sugar. The social system through which this aim has been realized has depended almost entirely on the agreements, conflicts, and balance of powers between forces that operate at the national level.

It should be noted that not all the conflicting ties in the structure of the plantation are of equal significance. Labour is the basic factor in the structure of the plantation. It is to be expected, then, that conflict involving labour, especially labour-management conflict, is of primary importance and influences conflicts occurring in other sectors of social activity. The following section, therefore, examines conflict between labour and management.

LABOUR AND MANAGEMENT

The central feature of this relationship is the labourer's sale of his labour power to management. This act of sale is governed by laws of supply and demand which determine the price that is offered and accepted. However, economic action, as Firth has pointed out,[1] occurs within a framework of 'concomitant social relations'. The organization of the labour market, and the values that govern preference within it, are conditioned by the social structure through which it operates.

The social framework most relevant to the study of conflict in this context is the distribution of power between the contracting parties. The wages actually paid are the outcome, over and above strictly economic factors, of a process of bargaining. The paradigm of this process is one in which two persons attempt to come to an agreement while, at the same

[1] Firth, 1951, ch. 4.

time, each seeks to maximize his gains at the expense of the other. Since conflict, according to the definition followed here, is action 'oriented intentionally to carrying out the actor's own will against the resistance of the other party or parties', and power, also by Weber's definition, is 'the chance of a man or a number of men to realize their own will in a communal action even against the resistance of others',[1] the relative distribution of power and the opposed interests between the contracting parties are the basic determinants of conflict in this relationship.

Organization for Disputes

During the indenture period the balance of power between labour and management was heavily weighted in favour of the latter. The legal order of society reinforced the employer's power to conclude the bargain according to his wishes and to penalize the labourer for resisting. The individual coolie was totally powerless. Both the indentured and the free coolies were tied to the plantation. For most of them, besides legal restrictions, there were no avenues of either vertical or horizontal mobility which enabled them to escape from their status in the plantation system. Except for a handful of drivers, few were able to rise on the plantation beyond the status of labourer. Moving out of the plantation was prevented by the labour laws (for indentured labourers) and by lack of capital (for the free ones). The coolies therefore had to protect their own interests on the plantations. The only way they could do so was to form themselves into a tightly knit group and counterbalance the power of management by a complete unanimity in opposition.

This close association was not achieved through any formal organization, for no trade unions existed or were allowed to exist. There were no political parties through which the labourers could make their demands felt. Unity of the group was achieved through an informal process of self-identification. This was possible because (a) the isolation of the coolies and their deviant culture enhanced the cohesion of the group, and (b) the organization of the labour force ironed out traditional social distinctions and emphasized their equality; as coolies a low political and social status was common to them all, so that each labourer was the equal of any other in social status and power.

The social equivalence of all coolies was the organizational principle of social solidarity in the bargaining process. Since all were alike, they all acted in concert. There was little differentiation of function and leaders were accepted only for ad hoc purposes. One of several equally qualified and acceptable persons might be given authority to act as spokesman for expressing grievances in a particular situation, but the leader in one such situation was not the leader in the next, and consequently there was a rapid succession of leaders. Delegation of authority was never permanent enough for a definite structure of authority to emerge. A permanent leadership would, in any case, have driven a wedge into the unity of the group.

[1] Weber, 1958, p. 180.

There was a more specific reason for the absence of a regular leadership. Jenkins, among others, reported that labourers were averse to sending representatives to negotiate because representatives 'became marked men, and were likely to be persecuted, whereas if they all came together the danger was distributed'.[1]

Consequently in most disputes with management the coolies acted *en masse*. Strikes tended to spread with lightning rapidity through the whole labouring population. Complaints to magistrates and the Immigration Department were made by whole gangs. Jenkins described such an incident as follows:

I found the road and the garden occupied by about three hundred Indians. ... They had their hoes, shovels and cutlasses, and were covered by the dingy marks of toil. A dispute had occurred with the manager of the estate, whereupon they had struck, and come down to ask Mr Des Voeux to help.[2]

It is interesting to note that in this, as in other reported instances, the coolies carried their work implements. It suggests the ceremonial character of social action in a mechanically solidary group.

Such concerted action was the cause of many riotous assemblies leading to shooting by the police. Indeed, in the absence of any satisfactory formal representation of their interests, minor wage disputes tended to become major clashes involving several hundred people.

For instance, in 1871, a wage dispute at Plantation Devonshire Castle, in Essequibo, led to a serious disturbance in which the Riot Act was read and the police shot five labourers dead.[3] At the inquest the manager testi-fied that coolies came in a group of about 140 to ask for higher wages. He refused to grant this increase and they went away in a body to the magis-trate to whom they reported their grievances. In addition, two labourers laid a complaint of assault against the manager. According to the testimony of the magistrate's clerk, when the case was called for hearing three days later, three hundred coolies were present in the compound of the court-house. They were not satisfied with the court's procedure, walked out in a body and returned to the plantation where they formed a human barricade across the entrance. They refused to let anyone pass through and demanded that the magistrate hold court before them on the road, this being the only assurance of justice they were prepared to accept. They refused to disperse on the reading of the Riot Act and the police fired. This incident was typical of all the other coolie disturbances which erupted periodically during the indenture period.

Indenture was abolished in 1917. The trade union movement began in British Guiana in 1919 with the formation of the British Guiana Labour Union by Hubert Critchlow. This union organized the urban labourers for the most part, but it took an interest in plantation labourers too. Its activities in plantations were severely limited by the managers' opposition

---

[1] Jenkins, 1871, p. 112.   [2] ibid., p. 104.   [3] *Report*, 1872.

to their labourers joining the union. Writing in 1939, J. D. Tyson, an emissary of the Indian Government, remarked:

Up to the time I left the Colony the M.P.C.A.[1] had not been recognized by the Sugar Producers' Association, and there is reason to believe that its branch secretaries and members had been to some extent subject to victimization on the estates. The Sugar Producers refused to recognize what they chose to consider an irresponsible and subversive body which, they believed, did nothing but organize trouble on the estates.[2]

What was true in 1939 was also true during the inter-war period. Even after the abolition of the indenture system, the coolies' protection of their interests continued to take the form of a large body of people acting in concert. Tyson pointed out that, with the abolition of the indenture system, the coolies lost the only formal organization which, up to a point, looked after their interests, the Immigration Department.

For instance the police shooting at Ruimveldt in 1924 was caused by about 4,000 coolies and Negroes starting to 'march on Georgetown with a band and flags, and armed with heavy sticks and agricultural implements',[3] some to meet Critchlow at the B.G. Labour Union and others to the Immigration Department, to complain about insufficient wages. That this was still a regular occurrence is seen in the testimony, under cross-examination, of a driver:

I have seen them go to the Crosby[4] since 1917. Usually the whole gang goes. . . . I have often seen them go to the Crosby; they take their tools, shovels, sticks and cutlasses as they leave the estate.[5]

The assembly refused to send delegates or disperse on the reading of the Riot Act and the police fired. The desire to meet Critchlow indicates that some coolies were making use of the unions. Still, even in 1935, though the B.G. Labour Union was associated with the wave of strikes which swept the country, it did not organize them. These strikes were 'spontaneous, widespread and determined'.[6]

The Position of the Union

The first union of specifically sugar plantation labourers was the Man-Power Citizens' Association (M.P.C.A.), founded in 1937 by two Indians, C. R. Jacob and Ayub Edun. The union found the task of organizing the labourers easy because of the existing solidarity among them. Lewis noted that:

It has had remarkable success in organizing the agricultural workers. East Indian agricultural labourers have proved easier to organize than Negro workers. They have a great sense of national solidarity, being bound together by their own languages, religions and social customs.[7]

[1] The Man-Power Citizens' Association, a union mainly of sugar workers.
[2] Tyson, 1939, p. 15.   [3] *Report*, 1924, p. 15.   [4] See n. 2 on p. 11 above.
[5] *Report*, 1924, p. 15.   [6] Lewis, 1939, p. 17.   [7] ibid., p. 18.

But the M.P.C.A., as Tyson noted, was not recognized by the employers, and its representatives were not permitted to enter the plantations. Industrial disputes continued to be dramatized by mass action until the shootings at Plantation Leonora in 1937 and at Plantation Enmore in 1948 impressed on employers the necessity for labour organizations. The M.P.C.A. had been formally recognized by the Sugar Producers' Association as far back as 1939 but the managements of individual plantations had continued to stamp out union activities within their domains. It was not until 1949, when the proposals of the Venn Commission, which stressed the need for a workable system of collective bargaining, including official union representation, were accepted by the Government and the Sugar Producers' Association, that the union became established in the plantations. The implementation of these proposals led to the resurrection of the Joint Committees, consisting of representatives of labourers and management, which had been instituted about three years earlier. The Union and the Labour Department were invited to send advisers and observers and were kept informed of proceedings. This is the situation as it exists today.[1]

The acceptance of the union by management has lessened but not eliminated the necessity for mass action. There are no more public demonstrations and marches on towns, at least on the same scale, but action as a group continues to be a feature of industrial disputes. The full examination of this problem merits a separate study. Here I shall discuss a few of the more important contributory factors.

Plantation labourers tend to be strongly antagonistic to all who are in positions of authority in matters concerning their economic and political interests. This antagonism, as already mentioned, was bred by the pressure of the indenture and inter-war periods and subsists on present clashes. It is a strongly entrenched tradition, a built-in bias in the interpretation of men and events. That the whole social order rests on 'de punishment of de black and coolie people' is an axiom in the ideology of plantation labourers, and is emphasized by speaker after speaker at strike meetings and informal discussion groups. That management and clerks cheat and hold back wages, that overseers and drivers overwork and ill-treat labourers, that the police institute trumped-up charges, that magistrates dispense justice only for the rich, that civil servants are slothful hypocrites, that doctors do not care whether their patients die, that lawyers are 'lying sharks', that politicians are opportunist and corrupt—all these views are solemnly averred in innumerable contexts. The basic principles of the administration of society are bribery, nepotism and exploitation; its motive forces are malice and lust for gain and the chief victims of this iniquitous system are the plantation labourers.

Castigation is directed at established authority and any organization or person associated with it. On the other hand, all organizations and persons opposed to it receive a ready approval. For example, the British Guiana

[1] See *Report*, 1949, for a fuller account of Joint Committees.

East Indian Association, in the days when it could be an effective vehicle for the ambitions of Indian politicians (campaigning on an 'Indianist' ticket), used to associate itself with the cause of the plantation labourers. But its leadership was rejected utterly at the Ruimveldt incident when its officials associated themselves with the police in urging the coolies to disperse. They were manhandled by the crowd for being 'paid officers of the government' and were rescued by the police.[1]

This was probably the last time the B.G.E.I.A. espoused the cause of the labourer. Indianist politicians continued on the political scene until the overwhelming victory of the left-wing and multi-racial P.P.P.[2] in the 1953 elections. Since then, to my knowledge, no politician, Indian or Negro, arguing for the advancement of a particular ethnic group in terms of its own cultural interests and values, and not advocating a programme of radical economic and political reform, has been elected in the plantation areas. The rejection of the leadership of the B.G.E.I.A. and Indianist politicians may be attributed to another closely associated factor. Following Epstein's analysis[3] of the rejection of the Tribal Elders by African copper miners in Rhodesia, one may conclude that, as labourers, the coolies saw themselves as participating in a social system distinct from that in which they participated as members of the 'Indian community'. They accord the cultural leaders of the community (mainly philanthropic business men and successful professionals) authority and prestige in activities concerning Indian culture, but choose other leaders in political and trade union activities.

But the recognition of the union by management may be described as a kiss of death. The remarkable support which the M.P.C.A. received at its inception diminished rapidly in the years following its recognition.[4] The Agreement signed by the M.P.C.A. and the Sugar Producers' Association, which formed the basis of the recognition, is interpreted as an act of collusion. Very few labourers in either Blairmont or Port Mourant have actually read the Agreement which, in its broad outlines, is of the usual kind signed by employers and unions. Their ignorance does not prevent them talking about villainous intentions concealed in its clauses, and even of bribery as inducement to their leaders to agree. Such beliefs may seem reasonable to those who hold them and yet they often lack solid foundation. For example, imperial honours awarded to union officials are sometimes interpreted as confirmation of their suspicions. Consequently when the P.P.P. started the Guiana Industrial Workers Union it was received by the plantation labourers with great acclaim. Its non-recognition

---

[1] *Report*, 1924, pp. 15 et seq.
[2] The People's Progressive Party. It started as a completely multi-racial party, but has since split into an Indian-dominated party (P.P.P.) and a Negro-dominated party (P.N.C.). However, both parties are overtly non-racial and wage their controversy in terms of political and economic issues without reference to race.
[3] Epstein, 1958, ch. 4.   [4] Jagan, 1954, pp. 50-63.

by the Sugar Producers, who prefer to deal with the M.P.C.A., has increased the popularity of the former and the unpopularity of the latter. Since one of the last acts of the deposed P.P.P. government of 1953 was to try to force the recognition of the G.I.W.U., many plantation labourers are firmly convinced that it was this attempt to give them the leadership they desired which led to charges of communist subversion, the suspension of the constitution and the arrival of British troops. To this day there is a strong under-current of animosity towards the M.P.C.A. and a readiness to believe that union officials are in the pay of management, or are seeking employment with them. For example the institution of the 'check-off', the system by which management co-operated in the deduction of union dues from wages, was readily interpreted as another sign that the union was in league with management.

An example of this antagonism was the labourers' conduct at a meeting arranged by the union to present its plans for dealing with rising unemployment. The meeting was scheduled to start at 5.30 p.m., but the union leaders were late. Criticism of its leaders, speculation about their betrayal of the labourers' interests, and examples of their opportunism were widely discussed by the waiting crowd. There was considerable scepticism about whether the union would do anything, and the general opinion appeared to be that the plans were merely attempts 'to fool de people'. Tension mounted until at last the union leaders arrived by car, two hours late. A lamp was lit, a table and microphone installed, and the meeting began. But it did not last for more than a few minutes, for the speakers were interrupted first by hecklers and then by stones and bottles. The union leaders packed up their microphones and departed amidst the jeers of the crowd.[1]

The distrust of the M.P.C.A. is one reason for the active participation of the whole group in industrial disputes. While there is a certain delegation of authority, a countervailing antagonism limits the readiness to accept the decisions of leaders. This applies to union leaders and even more to leaders drawn from among the labourers themselves. That leaders betray is an axiom. Conferences of delegates with management are unpopular. Labourers prefer to be present at negotiations, not necessarily as spokesmen but at least as silent watchdogs of their own interests. The closeting of delegates with the manager raises serious doubts as to whether some horse-deal is not being concluded behind closed doors.

This scepticism has its causes. There have been cases of union officials accepting jobs with the Sugar Producers' Association. Local labour leaders are, sometimes, won over by soft jobs and privileges. It is unlikely that this happens regularly, but the occasional occurrence is sufficient to reinforce the sceptical attitude.

---

[1] It should be pointed out that this is not the usual reaction to the union. It is an extreme expression of a prevalent tendency which is reinforced by the fact that the union is largely organized from the top and its leaders are mostly of urban middle status.

In these circumstances local leaders tend to be of the charismatic type. Frequent failures make their leadership short-lived. Of the eleven leaders who contested seats in the Blairmont Joint Committee in 1956, only four contested the elections in 1957. Of the seven who were successful in 1956 only three were popular enough to gain seats in 1957. Again, only two persons whose names appear among the labourers' representatives in minutes of Joint Council meetings in 1950–3, are still on the scene as active or potential leaders.

The rapid circulation of leadership positions is also deeply influenced by the egalitarian ideology. To some extent the leadership of outsiders, of P.P.P. and M.P.C.A. officials, is accepted. But with regard to members of the same community, that one person is abler than others or that he should act as leader in all trade disputes is not generally accepted. Labourers in both the shovel and cane-cutting gangs, when asked why several persons acted as their spokesmen in their trade disputes, replied that many wished to be spokesmen and that all should be given a chance, even though they conceded, in theory and for the purposes of argument, that some were abler than others. Consequently, many men have acted as leaders at some time or other, but no-one has been leader for long.

Another factor which limits the effectiveness of unions, and so inhibits the growth of an effective leadership, is the method of computing wages for agricultural labour, especially in the unskilled grades. Wages for all categories of labour, whether payment is by time or by piece-rate, are at standard rates enforced by the Labour Department. Demands for an increase of the standard rates or reduction of working hours account for only a small proportion of industrial disputes. But these standard rates have been arrived at on the hypothetical basis of average tasks and average working conditions. They hold good for the more controllable working conditions of the factory but are frequently not applicable in the field. For instance, cane-cutters are paid at a fixed rate per ton of cane cut under average conditions. But actual conditions can vary a great deal: rain makes cutting the cane difficult, a new variety of cane may be lighter than the one usually grown, the ground may be soggy with rain, the terrain may be uneven, the undergrowth may be thick, the punts for loading the cane may be delayed and the labourers compelled to wait for them, a shortage of punts may make it necessary to keep the cane in the field overnight which, the cane-cutters believe, reduces its weight, some cane may be carelessly transported to the factory and so lost on the way. Any of these factors may lead to demands for additional payment and require investigation on the spot. The same applies to weeders, fork-men and shovel-men.

All this provides fertile ground for disputes in which quick decisions are necessary. Resorting to the machinery of unions and joint consultations before taking action can be detrimental to the labourers. Labourers who cut the cane while negotiations about their claim for extra pay are proceeding, may find that they have finished the job before the decision has been made, and then the Company's negotiators can ask them to take or leave the offer. The union's undertaking not to call a strike until all attempts to reach agreement have failed is not always feasible. Decisions, especially to strike, have often to be made on the spot and without recourse to long deliberations.

A labourer has little chance of winning his case if he is arguing only for himself. But if he can show that he is speaking for all or most of the gang, his bargaining position is much stronger. A strong solidarity, based on an unquestioned identification of interests, facilitates such action. In all strikes observed in the field there was hardly any prior discussion. The word to strike passed rapidly across the field. Each man looked up and hesitated and a few shouldered their tools and left the field. This was a crucial moment for, unless the others joined, the strike would have failed. Occasionally it happened that the first to leave the field found themselves alone or that a few continued to work after most had left. But usually the majority left the field without much consultation and returned in a body to the office for further negotiations.

Sometimes everyone knew what the strike was about, sometimes many did not. The only reason some could give was that 'Ah we all strike. So me come away.' Occasionally explanations of the cause of the strike differed. Yet to describe this as 'mob psychology' is to misunderstand the situation. Those who argued with the overseer and the driver about the rate of pay, and those who heard them, knew the cause of the strike. But working conditions can differ from one part of the field to another and the perception and assessment of obstacles are partly subjective. Consequently, the initial reaction to the announcement of the rate may differ from one labourer to another or from one part of the field to another. Some may be readier to accept it than others, but if the latter are sufficiently determined to cease work, the rest will also down tools. For the sentiment that each one should 'support *mati*' is strong, and this support is given before making detailed inquiries as to the cause at issue. The bonds of *mati* require this.

Further, it is generally accepted that all strikes are 'for price', and most labourers are ready to strike for this. When obstacles affect all, even those who were not present at the bargaining know exactly why they are striking. Most labourers, as soon as they reach the field, survey working conditions with a sharp and practised eye to detect obstacles.

Antagonism to leaders, to the government, to management, and to the union, is only one aspect of the relations between the labourers, severally and as a group, and the total society. It is therefore necessary to examine industrial disputes from other aspects.

INDUSTRIAL DISPUTES

I have pointed out that opposition is implicit in the bargaining relationship between labourers and management. It is equally important to note that both sides are, ultimately, anxious to reach a settlement. There is basic agreement between the opposed groups that sugar production must continue. One of the most powerful arguments of those who wished to wean the plantation labourers from the P.P.P. during the 1953 elections was that the leaders of that party sought 'to destroy the sugar industry and to pull down the sugar chimneys'.[1] These charges, repeated during the 1957 elections, caused much discussion among the labourers. The labourers of Port Mourant attribute the closing of the factory to a desire to 'punish de poor people'. That both management and labourers have a stake in the industry is clearly stated in a resolution passed at a strike meeting. This resolution was the most serious expression of hostility to management I observed; it categorically demanded the removal of an official:

(a) Whereas shortly after the appointment of Mr X——— there started to exist a feeling of ill-relationship between the said [official] and the majority of the factory workers, due to the [official's] continuous use of abusive, insultive and indecent language to workers and refusal to negotiate with the representatives,

(b) And whereas the attitude of the [official] has been the result of the factory representatives having to take the matter to the Administrative Manager on two occasions,

(c) And whereas despite an assurance from the Administrative Manager that there would be good relationship between the [official] and the workers and for their representatives, the ways of the [official] remained unchanged,

(d) And whereas on account of the bitter feelings between the [official] and the workers, there is bound to exist non-co-operation in the factory,

(e) And whereas non-co-operation in the factory is also bound to cause disturbances, ruin and suffering to all workers, and also to its directors and shareholders, in that production, wages and profits would all tend to be lowered,

(f) Be it resolved that in view of the serious circumstances facing the factory and the industry, this mass meeting ... demands from the Administrative Manager his immediate recommendation to the Sugar Producers' Association for the earliest removal of this [official]. ...

The sophisticated wording of this resolution was the work of one of the abler representatives of the Joint Committee and an experienced trade unionist. But the sentiments expressed in the clauses were voiced by several speakers at the meeting as well as by the audience. Labourers are as much interested as management in expanding production, for they recognize that this means increased employment and wages. Incentive bonuses for the achievement of production targets institutionalize this common interest. Targets and achievements are chalked up on a score-board outside the factory.

To state the obvious, a certain minimum agreement on types and

[1] Jagan, 1953, p. 17.

standards of work, working hours, rates of pay, and the obligation to provide a 'fair wage' are a prerequisite for the organization of the labour force even on a semi-voluntary basis. Associated with this is acceptance of the structure of authority represented by managers, overseers, and drivers. The system of production cannot work without a set of conventions accepted by both labour and management.

The labourers take an interest in the plantation and its reputation. In Blairmont, for instance, labourers inform visitors that the plantation is reputed to have the best Senior Staff Compound in British Guiana. Certain standards of workmanship are accepted by both sides. For example, when asked to name the best labourers in the shovel gang, a manager and several labourers named the same four persons. The prowess of a driver in Port Mourant, promoted to this position because of his remarkable strength and efficiency as a cane-cutter, was talked about throughout the district even though he had ceased to cut cane forty years earlier. Several older men described their personal worth in terms of their service to the plantation: 'Me work plough, cutlass and shovel all over dis estate.' There is a widespread interest in the machinery of the plantation, irrigation techniques and cultivation plans. Given the rates of pay, there are clear notions as to what a fair day's work and fair wages are. Among the labourers too, certain individuals are described as 'lazy' and 'slackers'.

Co-operation on the basis of these common interests is regulated by certain norms. Disputes arise from disagreement as to (a) which norms should apply in a given situation and (b) whether a certain act is a deviation from a norm or not. Labourers and management adopt conflicting interpretations of the norms, each side advancing the view most advantageous to itself. A consideration of some events which led to strikes in Blairmont exemplifies this point.

The following dispute arose from a disagreement as to which norm should be held to apply:

Ramsujit was a driver in charge of a gang of female labourers who stitched sugar bags. It was alleged that he had seduced two of these women. The factory labourers reported him to management. An inquiry was held, Ramsujit was found guilty, removed from his post, and suspended for a month. At the end of this period he was sent to act as foreman of the dock workers. The latter, supported by the factory workers, protested against his appointment to any supervisory post. Management insisted on its right to employ him as it considered fit. The workers came out on strike.

The disciplinary action taken with regard to the driver made no reference to his future employment. The labourers insisted that he should not be employed in any supervisory capacity at all; management's view was that he should be debarred only from a position in which he might repeat his offence. Eventually management 'agreed' with the labourers and employed him in the laboratory. Soon there was another dispute as to whether this new job was 'supervisory' or not.

The second dispute turned on whether a given act or decision was a deviation from the norm or not:

Fork-men used to be paid at the rate of 7½ cents per rod[1] for each bed they cleared and planted. Management introduced a new method of planting which changed the nature of the work somewhat. The fork-men claimed that this change entailed more labour and that they should now be paid at the rate of 10 cents per rod. Management admitted that the nature of the work had changed, but contended that the amount of labour involved was the same.

In this case the issue was whether or not the new method entailed more than the normal amount of effort. The labourers argued that, at the normal pace of work, a fork-man could no longer earn his expected wage. Management agreed that a fork-man should earn his normal wage, but denied that, under the new method, he would have to expend more labour in earning it.

The nature of agricultural work is such that it continually presents new situations which demand new solutions. Established practices have to be constantly re-defined in new contexts. Moreover conditions in the labour market may change, the cost of living may have risen; these and similar factors can contribute to produce a dispute.

The norms that could govern each new situation are known to both sides. Each selects a position that is both advantageous and defensible, for the dispute is waged with a view to a negotiated settlement. Neither side is intractable for long. Industrial conflict arises from the organizational problem[2] of deciding which norms and precedents should be chosen as most desirable. Given the fact that each side seeks to maximize its advantage, the choices it makes can result in a clash of interests. But the dispute is waged within a social system which, in its broad essentials, is accepted by both sides. Conflict arises in those parts of the system which are elastic enough to permit each side to manipulate a situation to its own advantage.

IDEOLOGY OF THE LABOURERS

Disputes with management are of basic importance in the lives of all plantation labourers and therefore the solidarity of the group is one of the basic concerns of the local community. It is only in the last decade that this solidarity has been achieved, though only partially, through the formal organization of the trade union, the Joint Committee and negotiation through representatives. In the past it arose from the consciousness of common status and thus of equal rights among all coolies. The values of *mati*, discussed in Chapter 3, lay down the sentiments and norms of behaviour which should prevail between members of the group.

I do not wish to suggest that egalitarian norms are produced by the necessities of disputes with management. The incidence of similar norms and values in sub-groups of a variety of societies suggests that they should be associated with a more general set of factors. But egalitarian norms

[1] One rod = 14 feet.   [2] Firth, 1955.

fulfil certain functions in such disputes as are inevitable and central to the acting out of the labourer's role and, in turn, these disputes sharpen the awareness of being *mati*.

These norms and values may, following Parsons' definition,[1] be described as an ideology; it is, firstly, a set of beliefs concerning the nature of the group and 'the situation in which it is placed'. The labourers occupy a low social status in the stratification of the plantation as well as in that of the wider society. They have few of the qualities and qualifications which confer power and prestige in the society. Education, income, property, and style of life mark them out as a distinct and relatively homogeneous social group. They see themselves as under-privileged. They are all placed in the same situation of subordination and opposition to management. They regard their failure to attain desired advantages as 'punishment', which they recognize as the fate of all coolies. Most of them are unskilled and occupationally undifferentiated.

They are also a residential group and interact in a wide range of activities. Friends, kinsmen, and neighbours who co-operate at ceremonies are also fellow-labourers. Housewives are in and out of one another's houses and children of neighbours are fed if present at meal-times. Family ties bind several labourers into close groups and collateral and affinal ties link several such groups. The widespread use of such courtesy kinship terms as 'uncle' and 'auntie' enmeshes practically the whole local group. 'Coolie custom' gives a general validity to the egalitarian ideology. Through it the consciousness of being 'all de same' is extended beyond the social status, occupational, and kinship contexts.

Secondly, 'Subscription [to the ideology] is institutionalized as part of the role of collectivity membership'.[2] Acceptance of the ideology makes unity in action possible even though there is no explicit organization for co-ordinating behaviour. Social action in disputes with management requires the unquestioned assumption of community of interests. The strength of the labourers' cause depends on unanimity and, in the absence of any mechanism for ensuring this, mechanical solidarity. Thus the performance of the role of labourer enjoins behaviour in accord with the norms of being *mati*. And because the relations between labourers are not limited to the work situation, acceptance of these tenets as the norms for a variety of social relations becomes obligatory.

SOCIAL HOMOGENEITY AND SOCIAL DIFFERENTIATION

The egalitarian ideology produces a sharper awareness of some features of the social system. It emphasizes common subordination to management, common residence, common descent and culture, kinship ties, similarity of opportunity and style of life. All these features underline the homogeneous aspect of the coolie group.

However, other features, such as differences in income and prestige,

---

[1] Parsons, 1951, pp. 349–50.   [2] ibid.

levels of achievement, membership in the community of the higher-status Junior Staff, and the like, are incompatible with the egalitarian ideology. These two aspects are in continuous friction and result in considerable ambiguity and tension in social relations. One example of this is the ambiguous position of the Junior Staff, who are distinguished from the labourers by a distinctive style of life, highly valued occupational and social skills, and regular incomes. They participate in the activities of the local community only to a limited extent. Their conditions of employment do not permit them to express overtly their solidarity with the rest of the community in industrial disputes. Social relations of Junior Staff personnel tend to become increasingly confined to themselves.

Nevertheless, there are important links between them and the labourers. They are not an endogamous group and, as Parsons has pointed out,[1] no system of social stratification is complete unless each group tends to be endogamous. Such restrictions are being developed and a senior clerk will prevent his daughter from marrying a labourer, but, at present, most Junior Staff persons are only first generation members of the group and are bound by kinship to labourer families. Labourer fathers, brothers, cousins and affines participate in their domestic ceremonies. Ties of neighbourhood and boyhood friendships as well as adherence to the same culture reduce the social distance between them and the labourers. Unless a member of the Junior Staff elects to cut himself off entirely, he still associates himself with the labourer group in some contexts.

The ambiguous position of being partly within the labourer group and partly out of it causes friction and leads to confusion in mutual expectations. With a growing crystallization of social status distinctions the Junior Staff will become a more closed group. When this happens it may be expected that Junior Staff–labourer antagonism will change in character and probably become less acute.

Distinctions between skilled and unskilled labourers are less marked. Skilled labourers are much less able to withstand pressures to conform to egalitarian norms. There is no formal recognition of their superiority and no institutions, such as the Junior Staff Club, to dissociate them from the wider group. Further, unlike the Junior Staff, skilled and unskilled labourers are allies in disputes with management. There is little overt friction between them.

Thus egalitarian norms do not apply equally to the behaviour of all. The Junior Staff is frequently exempt and a limited institutional differentiation enables them to withdraw from some contexts where such norms apply. Brahmin priests can, in certain contexts, assert their superiority and so can relatively wealthy shopkeepers and tradesmen. The norms apply mainly to the labourers who form the vast majority of the community, especially to the unskilled labourers.

But even within this group there are, in fact, socially important

[1] Parsons, 1954, pp. 69–88.

inequalities. The life chances of all labourers can, broadly speaking, be said to be similar, but within these limits differences in individual capabilities and opportunities produce inequalities and distinctions. The system of labour relations which creates a need for a strong solidarity of the group tends, at the same time, to atomize this solidarity through individual contracts of employment and individual assignment of work and rewards. Among unskilled labourers, and more so among skilled labourers, wages and regularity of employment differ. Except in certain sections of the factory there is very little interdependence at work. Varying capacities for work, strength, skill, and conscientiousness result in varying incomes. Though the informal structure of the work situation emphasizes the primacy of the group, the formal structure emphasizes the individual.

Again, the circumstances of one labourer differ from those of another. Some have larger families and more dependants and consequently higher expenses than others. Some may have prosperous relatives who help them to meet their obligations, find jobs for their sons, and augment their income in many ways. For instance, the offer of rice-lands, free or at a nominal rent, makes it possible to acquire symbols of success not normally accessible to the average labourer. Differing personalities too serve to accentuate these differing circumstances as well as the manner in which individuals meet them.

Socially relevant differences arise in non-economic activities also. A Brahmin or a Kshatriya has more prestige than a low-caste man. The kinsmen of a member of the Junior Staff, even though they themselves are labourers, share something of his prestige. A driver's relatives can expect preferential treatment in obtaining regular or better paid jobs. In religious activities organizing ability and knowledge of the ritual give some individuals more influence than others. Fluency in 'high English', ability to read, write and calculate give some persons prominent roles in industrial disputes.

Egalitarian norms prevail mainly within the context of the local community. In so far as labourers are members of the wider society, social action among them, as among other status groups, is geared to values of individual achievement and worth. The importance of regular employment, the prestige of a skilled occupation or a big income, the acquisition of culturally valued goods, prestige won by adopting, where possible, high social status manners, and the desire to raise the social status of one's children if not one's own—all these interests motivate the behaviour of labourers as well as other groups of the society. The symbols of success and individual worth are similar for all status groups, though the levels of aspiration and achievement differ.

An almost universal concern with success and the prestige gained from it gives rise to a process of competition which makes inroads into the solidarity of the group and runs counter to the presumption of social equality. Achievement and success in themselves do not conflict with the norms of the group. Achievement of Junior Staff status is widely applauded.

Local success stories are recounted with pride. Lawyers and doctors who come from plantation families are assured of a regular supply of clients from their home plantations because each is 'ah we boy'. Social mobility moves an individual beyond the range of *mati*. He leaves the local group altogether and his claims to greater prestige can be allowed without disappointing expectations or endangering the solidarity of the group.

But to claim a higher than average prestige within the labouring group, or to be suspected of doing so, leads sooner or later to conflict. Claims that are not backed by a higher social status are considered demonstrations of unjustified superiority. Prestige implies the expectation of a certain amount of deference which can be shown to a person of superior social status who is patently not *mati*. But a claim to superior prestige made by a person who belongs in all respects to the group frustrates the expectations of his fellows and undermines the solidarity of the group as a whole. The claim is contested and leads to the type of dispute which I shall examine in detail in the following chapter.

5

Disputes Over Prestige

An offence against the egalitarian norms is called an *eye-pass*.[1] The term is used in such expressions as 'You *eye-pass* me' or 'You take you eye and pass me.' It can be used as either a noun or adjective. Other parts of the anatomy, notably *rass*,[2] may be substituted for eye. To *eye-pass* someone is to offend his *amour propre*, to belittle and humiliate him, to ignore his rights and claims. The notion of lowering a man's dignity and prestige by repudiating what is justly his due is the essence of this term.

There are several other expressions besides *eye-pass* which emphasize the actor rather than the act: *take advantage 'pon, become biggity, play big, play bad, play manager, play white man, play mannish, play power-man, play braiga, play representer*,[3] etc., all express the view that to claim an unjustified superiority or control over another man lowers his prestige.

Except in rare cases where a whole group is explicitly provoked, an *eye-pass* occurs between individuals, and an act becomes an *eye-pass* only when the person at whom it is directed interprets it as an attempt to humiliate him.

For an action to be recognized as an *eye-pass* it is necessary for the persons involved to participate in a complex set of mutual obligations and interactions. Each is expected to meet his obligations in a manner which recognizes the equality of their respective statuses. Failure to fulfil an obligation is not necessarily an *eye-pass*, but deviation is frequently interpreted as an assumption of superiority. The following example illustrates some of the important ingredients of an *eye-pass*.

Example I

Balram and Kissoon were sons of two sisters. Balram's father was a driver and Kissoon's father was a fairly prosperous labourer who owned some land and several cattle.

Balram, like his father, became a driver. Kissoon and his brother, after a wild youth during which they spent their patrimony, settled down as shovel-men.

---

[1] I can shed no light on the etymology of this term except to point out the connotation of 'looking through' someone. The term appears to be peculiar to British Guiana.　　　　　　　　　　　　　　　　　　　　　　　[2] Arse.

[3] There is no agreed spelling of the language. I have followed the system used by the police when they record statements verbatim.

Balram rose high in the hierarchy of the plantation and became the most senior driver. He spared no expense in educating his children who entered the professions and became members of, or married into, relatively high-status groups (outside the plantation). His eldest daughter's marriage was notable for its sumptuousness and the galaxy of lawyers, doctors and overseers present.

Kissoon, though only a shovel-man, was energetic and capable. He was a leading figure in communal activities, both in the union and in the religious association.

One day Kissoon was passing by Balram's house when some of Balram's children jeered at him saying, 'Look it deh! A coolie-man ah pass!' Kissoon was incensed and upbraided them, asking them whether the schools in town did not teach them to respect their elders. They continued to taunt him.

He complained to Balram a few days later but the latter refused to hold himself responsible for his children's actions or apologize for them or promise to discipline them. Kissoon insisted that he had been wronged, but Balram replied that there was nothing he could do about it.

A few months later another of Balram's daughters was getting married. Balram sent Kissoon the customary prior notification given to kinsmen so that he could come to help. Kissoon read the message which was brought by one of Balram's sons and told the youth, 'Tell you father the coolie-man nah come. . . . Also tell you father, is a coolie-man, Jawarharlal, who rule India.'

The dispute between Balram and Kissoon arose out of the close relationship between them. In Kissoon's view, despite Balram's superior status, they were equals in prestige since they were cousins. But at the same time he suspected that Balram, because of his undoubted success in life, considered himself superior. As an elder kinsman Kissoon had a claim to respect and deferential behaviour from Balram's children. But, educated in the middle-status atmosphere of secondary schools, Balram's children saw Kissoon as a labourer rather than as an uncle and were anxious to repudiate the kinship link. In this situation Balram clearly had an obligation to discipline his children and restore to Kissoon the prestige due to him. He refused to do so and, by condoning his children's taunt of 'coolie-man' agreed that Kissoon was inferior. This was an *eye-pass*, for it denied Kissoon his due prestige and respect. Kissoon reacted by repudiating his obligation to help at the wedding. He felt this to be an effective retaliation for, through his influence in the community, he could have organized a considerable body of helpers. In his reply to Balram he contended that if they were not equals they could not behave as kin, and reminded him that they were both Indians and, in view of Nehru's achievement, there was no reason for Balram to repudiate their solidarity and equality as such.

Since there are no formal mechanisms for ensuring conformity to egalitarian norms, sanctions against *eye-pass* offences are diffuse rather than organized.[1] The agent of social control is the victim himself, and consequently much depends on the relative power of the offender and his victim

[1] Radcliffe-Brown, 1952.

to control each other's behaviour. Each person is the guardian of his own prestige.

Control of behaviour through informal processes depends on the degree of reciprocity between persons. A consideration of the social system of the plantation community makes it clear that, excluding management, one individual has very little power to control the actions of another. Each person is a member of the community by virtue of his relationship with management. Only within the family and in religious associations is there any formal interdependence between persons. Significantly enough, several marriages have been disrupted by offended affines persuading the offender's wife to leave him, and the activities of religious associations are marked by interminable disputes generated by personal animosities.

In the incident described above, Kissoon could retaliate by refusing to participate in the wedding. His conspicuous absence was noted by several persons who, when they discovered the reason, upheld his action and criticized Balram for 'playing braiga pon he cousin'. Thus Kissoon attracted public attention to his grievance and vindicated his prestige by obtaining its recognition through public sympathy. Similarly, when the president of the Jamaat[1] 'put out' his wife and took another, he was soon faced with votes of censure engineered by his wife's sister's husband, who had attempted to effect a reconciliation and had been abused and chased from the house. This was a breach of the norms of *mati*. The injured man retaliated by demanding the president's dismissal for misappropriation of funds and, when this failed, by successfully persuading a number of members to leave the Jamaat.

However, the number of persons who can be restrained by such methods is small. There are few institutions in the community whereby social control through reciprocity can operate. The relation between an individual and the community as a whole is different because he depends on it for a variety of needs. But even here, as will be shown, since each person's most important rights derive from his relation to management or to the wider society, the effectiveness of group sanctions is limited.

Nevertheless it should be noted that norms of *mati* are internalized in most individuals. To 'live good' and not to 'get story' with other persons are positive values. People pay each other exaggerated deference with such terms of address as *Captain* or *Cap, Skipper* or *Skip, Chief, Big Boy, Boss, Sadhu, Uncle,* etc. These terms are supposed to make the persons so addressed 'feel good'. On the other hand, where there is competition for prestige, the structuring of relationships admits few mechanisms for checking deviations from the egalitarian norms.

Consequently most attempts to control *eye-pass* offences, and sometimes even to commit them, take the form of violence, verbal or physical. The disputes discussed in this chapter are all quarrels involving some violence. There is a bias in favour of violent encounters because direct action is both

[1] Muslim association.

the most effective way of controlling *eye-pass*, and also the most observable. It is only after the underlying tension has exploded in action that neighbours—and the observer—realize and try to piece together the events which have led up to the final outburst. The quarrels described below, which were enacted before the public in house-yards and in the streets, are examples of the commonest expression of *eye-pass* disputes, and illustrate the significant characteristics of *eye-pass* and the manner in which the resultant disputes are waged.

BACKGROUND TO DISPUTES

Eye-pass can be committed in a variety of ways. It is often associated with the acquisition of symbols of wealth, for this causes some apprehension in others who feel their prestige threatened. The following example reflects a common pattern of events:

Example II

Ramdhani, a shovel-man, used to live in an old wooden house. The neighbouring group of five or six houses were somewhat, but not much, better than his own. Still there was one house in the neighbourhood which was considerably larger and better than the rest and this was occupied by Munidas, a watchman. (I should add that this incident occurred in a settlement of labour-owned houses.)

Munidas was older than the other household heads in this neighbourhood and considered himself, because of his greater age and affluence, the most important man in the vicinity. His neighbours tacitly acknowledged his position of *primus inter pares* and he reciprocated by allowing them to congregate in his yard for evening chats and inviting them to listen to news and sport commentaries on his radio. On the whole, relations among this group of neighbours, including Ramdhani, were amicable.

Then Ramdhani planned to get his daughter married in the following year and, in view of this, decided to build a new house. When the foundation pillars were laid it became clear to all that it would be bigger than Munidas's.

This annoyed Munidas, who suddenly demanded from Ramdhani an old plough he had given him a few years earlier and complained that the plough was returned to him damaged. He demanded compensation which Ramdhani refused to pay. Angry words passed between them. At harvest time Munidas used to thresh his paddy on Ramdhani's threshing ground. This year Ramdhani refused to allow Munidas to use it.

In time the house was completed. It had a green zinc roof and white walls. A linoleum with a bright floral design covered the floors and fretwork of a baroque style graced the lintels. Most of the windows were of frosted glass, a luxury associated with Senior Staff bungalows.

On the night the house was completed stones and bottles were thrown at it. Some window panes were smashed. Ramdhani rushed outside and claimed that he saw Munidas pelting the house. On the following night bottles were thrown again. Ramdhani went out with a stick and challenged Munidas. There was a fight between them, the police charged them both with assault and each was fined ten dollars.

Shortly after the case Ramdhani bought a seven-valve radio. This distressed Munidas sorely, for until now his had been the most powerful radio in the vicinity. Relations between them became worse than ever. A neighbour stated that, when Ramdhani passes by, Munidas stands by his gate 'throwing hints' to the effect that he is perfectly willing to go to court again. The neighbours tried to maintain good relations with both parties and even to mollify them. When the fight broke out the neighbours intervened to separate them.

Ramdhani's new house stood out like a monument in the neighbourhood. It was a challenge to Munidas whose prestige was now eclipsed by Ramdhani. This was an *eye-pass*; it was not committed by Ramdhani's having more wealth, which was unlikely, but by his using what he had in a manner that directly, or indirectly, lessened Munidas's prestige. Moreover Ramdhani had no basis for claiming greater prestige; he remained, like Munidas, an unskilled labourer and an Indian. The act of acquiring a seven-valve radio was not itself an *eye-pass*; but when it threatened to deprive Munidas of the crowd that gathered in his yard to listen to cricket and racing commentaries, it amounted to *eye-pass*. A series of acts—the building of a new house, the denial of any obligation to pay compensation, the refusal to allow use of the threshing ground, the purchase of a more powerful radio—considered as a meaningful sequence, confirmed, or was interpreted as confirming the impression that an *eye-pass* had been committed.

It was, in fact, this interpretation which sparked off the quarrel. Other neighbours did nothing to show that they regarded Ramdhani's new house as an *eye-pass* directed at them. They made genuine efforts to reconcile the opponents because they did not feel their positions to be immediately threatened. The new house did not undermine established expectations in their relations with Ramdhani; provided he continued to recognize their equivalent prestige by association in radio-listening and drinking parties, they could regard his achievement with equanimity. But Munidas could not react in the same manner because the grandeur of the new house and the new radio were an immediate threat to him. His expectations of the kind of behaviour due to him were denied. The only way he could apply sanctions through established relations was the feeble one of demanding the return of the plough. When this proved futile he resorted to violence.

Conflict of expectations is an essential element of *eye-pass* and an *eye-pass* dispute can be generated by a variety of circumstances. Objective evidence, such as the acquisition of superior social status symbols or conspicuous use of wealth is not necessary. A subjective impression that some slight has been offered, and an accumulation of such slights lead eventually to a violent climax the antecedents of which are often obscure, as in the following quarrel:

Example III

Harry and Dyal were neighbours; their houses, about twenty-five yards apart, faced each other across a canal. Harry's occupation was cleaning the plantation canals. It offered regular employment and, for unskilled work, good pay. Dyal was a shovel-man; he also owned a few cattle and rented two acres of rice in the village. Harry was a person of consequence in the Jamaat and Dyal was president of the Hindu church committee.

Harry was a heavy drinker and, when he was drunk, which was often, he was apt to boast of his importance and his superiority. His wife's brothers were important men in the area and he made much of this fact. A neighbour reported that relations between them had been cool for two or three years.

According to Harry, on the night the dispute reached a climax, he was at home with his wife scolding her for losing some money. While he was up-braiding her she heard Dyal call out from across the canal, 'Hi! Harry! Why you ah call me wife name in you mouth? You go pay dear for you mouth!' Harry looked out of the window and replied, 'Dyal, you take you eye and pass me; you really weigh me in you mind.' Dyal answered back, 'Me ah go and tell police now.' He walked some distance but returned, saying, 'Me ah come over and chop ah you f—— rass!' He went into his house, picked up a cutlass and waded across the canal. Harry's wife rushed out and he struck her with it.

Dyal's version was different. He heard his own wife's name mentioned and came out. He called another neighbour to witness how Harry was cursing his (Dyal's) wife saying that she 'took other men in bush'. His neighbour advised him to ignore it and so he returned home while Harry was still cursing and taunting him. He did not know how Harry's wife came by her wound.

Several neighbours had seen him wade across the canal with a cutlass and enter Harry's house, and heard Harry shout out that Dyal had wounded his wife. Dyal was charged by the police and fined.

In this incident, as in many others, it is difficult to disentangle fact from fiction, and even neighbours were in some doubt as to exactly what happened. Fortunately the truth of the matter is not relevant here; whatever version is true it may be concluded that one man *eye-passed* the other. Either Harry was speaking the truth and Dyal vaunted his superiority by bullying him, or Dyal was speaking the truth in saying that he was provoked. Several of the neighbours agreed that Harry had provoked Dyal by abusing the latter's wife and that Dyal must have wounded Harry's wife. The important question, however, is why Harry provoked Dyal by casting aspersions on his wife's virtue. Both Harry's provocative behaviour and Dyal's rash reaction are difficult to explain unless they are seen as the end-product of a series of acts committed by Harry with the intention of slighting Dyal and of a long-accumulated sense of grievance in the latter. Harry was addicted to bragging and insulting and much of his offensive behaviour was directed at Dyal. His last act in the series was so deliberate and public an attack that Dyal could not allow it to go unanswered.

The act which brings an *eye-pass* dispute to a head need not be in itself provocative. Such acts as chastising a neighbour's child or chasing away his fowl or dog, which are usually tolerated as harmless, can suddenly become the focus of a serious quarrel, as in the following example. The main part of the account is taken from police records, which consist of statements made by the accused and the constable who charged them with disturbing the peace.

Example IV

Gopal and Betta Boy were both unskilled field labourers. They were also neighbours sharing the same back fence. When Gopal obtained a regular job in the factory he was told that Betta Boy was spreading a rumour that he had obtained it by bribing the foreman and overseer. When Betta Boy contested the Joint Committee elections Gopal is supposed to have campaigned against him.

Two quarrels between them followed, both of which ended as cases in court. The first arose when Betta Boy's wife, Rukmin, accused Gopal's wife, Kausila, of killing her duck. Kausila retorted fiercely, they abused each other and both were fined in court.

The second quarrel broke out four months later and they were again charged by the police. The following statements were made in connection with this case.

The constable stated: '... I saw Kausila, Gopal and Rukmin quarrelling with each other. I heard Kausila saying to the top of her voice, "You child rass is not better than my own. You rass must take God out of you thoughts and strike him!" I heard Gopal saying in a loud tone of voice, "Who rass strong let we beat *mati* and go to the Station." Rukmin was saying, "Station nah make for dog. Any time me meet him pon de road me go beat he rass! "[1] All this was said in a loud tone of voice and a crowd gathered. I went up and spoke to them to stop their behaviour. They paid no attention to me but continued in the same manner. Kausila said I must not talk; if I want, let me carry them to the Station. I arrested them.'

Kausila stated: '... Rukmin started to complain to her husband telling 'um that me pickney[2] beat she pickney. She husband say, "Let dem go on. One of these days me go sleep in de Station for me pickney dem." Me turn round and tell dem it nah need all ah dat, dat pickney ah quarrel today and make up tomorrow. And Betta Boy say me must not talk at all; wha' he got in he mind he done get. Then me husband say, "Dat is nonsense." And Betta Boy say,"You better nah talk. Wha' me get in me mind me get already. When me done with all you de Station dere for me." Then me tell 'um de Station dere for justice.'

Rukmin stated: '... When me come home me pickney say that Kausila son beat he. ... When me husband come back six o'clock de child been get fever and he ask me wha' happen wid de child and me been telling 'um when Kausila hear and say, "It hurt you when me child beat you one, but me nah been carry me one ah doctor when you son beat 'um." Me ask she, "Why you nah been give me complain?" She tell me, "Me nah get no complain; who strong, so beat." She husband come out and say he nah get no satisfaction to give. Same time police been passing pon de road and shout on all we for keep quiet. And me keep quiet and dem continue. ...'

Gopal stated: '... Me been sitting down in me kitchen and me hear

[1] The word 'rass' is used here for emphasis; it adds little to the meaning but expresses a certain vehemence.

[2] 'Pickney' is derived from 'picaninny', meaning child.

Rukmin and Betta Boy ah quarrel. Dem say me child ah beat dem child. And Betta Boy say if he meet me child pon de road he go slap 'um. Me turn round and tell he, "When you ready to slap he you can slap he; then we go know better." Same time police been passing. . . .'

The background of competition between the protagonists of this dispute is seen in their attempts to deny each other their due prestige. When Gopal obtained a job in the factory, Betta Boy attempted to belittle his achievement by claiming that he obtained it through bribes. When Betta Boy contested a seat on the Joint Committee, Gopal worked against him to deprive him of a potential source of prestige. Their houses were about fifteen yards apart and therefore the Rukmin-Betta Boy conversation must have been conducted fairly loudly or else Gopal and Kausila must have been eavesdropping on their neighbours. According to an informed neighbour who maintained good relations with both sides, the duck died a natural death but Rukmin blamed Gopal and his wife because 'they get bad feelings', i.e. they were ill-disposed to each other. It was these 'feelings' which magnified the significance of the fight between their children. The competition between Gopal and Betta Boy conditioned their attitudes towards their children's quarrel: 'You child rass is not better than my own', 'Who rass strong let we beat *mati* and go to the Station.'[1] One child beating another was seen as a demonstration of superiority by its parents. Children run in and out of each other's homes and a neighbour may discipline someone else's child without giving its parents offence. But if there is a pre-existing antagonism such acts are invested with special significance. If anyone is expecting an affront he will find it in the most trivial and familiar occurrences.

There are several expressions for this state of armed peace. To get someone 'in mind' is one (e.g. Example III: 'You really weigh me in you mind'). To 'get feelings', to 'get story', to 'get old spite', to 'get worries', are others. This continuous state of cold war sometimes erupts in a series of incidents, one encounter tending to precipitate another. Thus the argument over the death of the duck soon led to the clash over the fight between children.

At this point it may be useful to review some of the general characteristics of the *eye-pass* disputes described so far.

In all four episodes there was an attempt, or a suspected attempt, by one person to detract from the prestige of another: Balram by condoning his children's offence, Ramdhani by building a bigger house and acquiring a more powerful radio, Gopal and Kausila by killing the duck and beating the child. Each of these instances, which confirmed that *eye-pass* was intended, was the end product of a series of acts which had been noted but not openly objected to. This is what is meant by 'getting feelings' or 'getting old spite'. This state of mind may exist in one protagonist, as in

[1] 'Your child is not better than mine', 'Whichever of us is stronger, let us beat each other and go to the Police Station.'

the dispute between Balram and Kissoon, or in both, as in the dispute between Gopal and Betta Boy. The intention to *eye-pass* may be present as in the case of Harry, or absent as in the case of Gopal's killing the duck, or it may be only an inference, as in the case of Ramdhani's house and radio. But if such a state of mind exists, any one of a number of actions may provide grounds for making the protest.

Once it is decided to check the other person from deviating from the norm, the way in which this is done depends on the relations between the parties and the available opportunities. It may be done through institutions that bring the protagonists into effective relations with one another. Kissoon had an effective method for exercising a sanction against Balram's behaviour by conspicuously boycotting the wedding. On the other hand Munidas and Dyal had no real hold over Ramdhani and Harry respectively. Betta Boy, who believed that Gopal, having secured a factory job, considered himself superior, in retaliation circulated a rumour with, probably, little effect. Gopal opposed him at the elections and aggravated his grievance by killing his duck and beating his child. All these persons, who had no effective means of controlling their detractors, resorted to direct and violent forms of protest.

THE COURSE OF DISPUTES

There are certain recognized ways of confronting the offender with his offence so that, even at a late stage, a violent climax may be averted. This procedure is not very frequently followed but it is available if the contending parties are willing to negotiate.

In Example IV, when Kausila countered Rukmin by asserting that her child had been beaten too, Rukmin replied, 'Why you nah been give me complain?' To 'give complain' before taking any action is the proper procedure; the suspected offender is thus given the opportunity of assuring the offended person of his good intentions or explaining the reprehensible act in a satisfactory manner. He apologizes or performs an act of restitution which restores the relationship to its *status quo*, the state of being *mati*. This is called 'giving satisfaction'. In Example IV, for instance, Gopal is reported to have said that 'he nah got no satisfaction to give'. If he had heeded Rukmin's 'complain' that her child had been beaten and had given satisfaction the dispute would have ended, for the time being at least, in a peace with honour. Similarly, when Kissoon complained to Balram it was up to the latter to give satisfaction: but he decided against doing so.

The procedure of 'complain' and 'satisfaction' is a mechanism for resolving a dispute and protecting the prestige of the contenders at the same time. The refusal to give satisfaction precipitates the violent climax, and this is apt to happen, for the 'complain' may be regarded as just one more infringement of one's prestige, an attempt to intimidate. In such a case the person making the 'complain' has no alternative but to declare open hostility. Sometimes the 'complain' is made as a peremptory demand. In

Example III Dyal did not complain about Harry's slander in a manner calculated to reach a settlement—'Why you ah call me wife name in you mouth? You go pay dear for you mouth!' The vehemence of the complaint was due to his certainty that Harry intended a deliberate *eye-pass*. Similarly, when a complaint is made so violently it is difficult for the other contender to give satisfaction; peace with honour is no longer possible. Harry rebutted Dyal's 'complain' with equal vehemence: 'You take you eye and pass me; you really weigh me in you mind.'

When it becomes clear to the wronged person that no satisfaction can be obtained, or if he thinks it futile to ask for it, he retaliates by abuse sometimes followed by assault. This is payment in kind, for to be abused in public is itself an *eye-pass* difficult to ignore. An unresponsive opponent may be taunted with such remarks as, 'Hi! Is you me ah talk to! You dog, you nah shame? Me go beat you rass today. . .', etc. If a man fails to reply to such challenges it is taken as an indication that he does not have to be treated with respect, and that in fact his prestige is so low that he dare not answer; or else that he fears the truth of the abuse. Indeed, most people, when they are abused in this way, are afraid of the onset of a series of public aspersions of their character and good name which will cause their prestige to sink to the bottom of the scale. However, most people are prone to 'get into one passion' when they are addressed in an abusive manner, without being goaded by such considerations. The reluctance to remain silent in the face of such challenges may perhaps explain the frequent defiance of policemen who attempt to pacify the contenders:

Example V

Telegram was told that his neighbours had said that he stole their fowls. One Saturday night he got drunk and shouted at the top of his voice: 'Dem f—— rass say me teef dem fowl, but dem take dem eyes pass me. And dem can go tell de police and when me get de f—— summons, me go f—— dem from one side. All me both side neighbour are Judas. When dem rass ah talk me name dem can't let me hear because I goin' burst dey rass and pay for um. Me get money for pay at court.'

When a constable, attracted by the din, ordered him to keep quiet, he replied: 'Me rass nah work ah field; me rass ah plant provision, so all you rass can't spite me!' The constable threatened to take him to the Police Station. Telegram backed into his house, locked the door and replied, 'Me goin' nowhere. If you want me, come for me!'

Telegram was an unskilled field labourer. His assertion, 'Me rass nah work ah field' was a claim to the superior status of farmer, the implication being that he was no ordinary 'back-dam worker' and therefore could not be insulted with impunity either by his neighbours or by the police.

THE ROLE OF THE PUBLIC

An *eye-pass* dispute is essentially one which is argued before the public. If a man wishes to assault someone who has offended him he does not do

so in private but before an assembled crowd, and the loud torrent of
invective which may last, intermittently, well up to half an hour is a means
of attracting a crowd and appealing to the public. The quarrels in Examples II and IV were enacted in the midst of an assembly summoned in
this manner. When Rukmin first hurled her abuse only I and three others
were standing on the dam a few yards away. By the time the police arrived
on the scene the succession of outbursts had attracted at least twenty-five
or thirty people. Even though no audience is actually attending, the abuse
and accusations are shouted aloud so that everyone in the neighbouring
houses can hear everything quite clearly. The acrimonious debate in
Example III was conducted typically between Dyal standing by his gate
and Harry about twenty-five yards away on the landing of the stairway to
his house. Alternatively a man may take his stand in front of his opponent's
house and harangue him aloud, calling him by name so that there is no
doubt as to whom he is addressing. The following example provides an
instance:

Example VI

Ishmael and Nasruddin were brothers. Amir was their father's sister's son.
Hassan was Amir's wife's brother. They were all cane-cutters.

Ishmael's father and Amir's father were not on very good terms. The
former, a fairly prosperous cultivator of rice (in addition to being a shovel-
man) had wished to buy a tractor, and had asked the latter for a contributory
loan. The latter replied he had no money, while the other accused him of
refusing the loan out of spite, and was particularly incensed when he was
advised not to bite off more than he could chew. Many years before, Amir's
father had accused Ishmael's father of withholding his sister's share of their
father's property. The strained relations between the parents appeared to
continue among their children.

A few weeks before the present incident a girl had cited Nasruddin as the
father in a bastardy case. He denied paternity, though there seemed little
doubt in the community that he was the father. The evidence at court went
against him; he lost the case and was ordered to pay for the upkeep of the
child. Since the case was heard a few days before his marriage to another girl,
Nasruddin and his whole family were deeply embarrassed by the decision
of the court.

During the rice harvest Ishmael and Nasruddin were working in their
father's field. The adjoining field was worked by Mahadeo on whose evidence
the case against Nasruddin had mainly rested. Mahadeo and Amir were
partners in working their fields and spent alternate days helping each other.

Ishmael and Nasruddin were threshing their paddy within earshot of
where Mahadeo and Amir were threshing theirs. Nasruddin said aloud, 'In
this world you cannot trust anyone.' Mahadeo responded to the challenge, a
heated argument arose, and Nasruddin charged Mahadeo with a pitchfork.
Amir held him and took the pitchfork away. Nasruddin turned on Amir and
asked him since when he was 'playing represeter' (i.e. when he had acquired
a high and official status which enabled him to control the actions of others).
Amir replied that he was wrong to attack Mahadeo, and what was more, he

was wrong to get the girl with child and not marry her. Ishmael was a silent witness of the proceedings.

That evening when he was at home, Amir heard Ishmael challenging him to fight. Ishmael was standing on the dam across the canal which ran by Amir's house. Ishmael poured out his invective for some time. Amir came out and said, 'If you call me a damned rass me come over the trench and cut your rass.' Ishmael replied, 'You can't do me one rass. You think you can play power-man.' Hassan joined the dispute by warning Ishmael and Nasruddin to disperse before he 'tended' to them. They defied him and included him in their invective. Ishmael shouted, 'Amir, you tek you eyes to pass me, but you wife is a whore!' Amir and Hassan crossed the canal and a fight between the four men broke out.

Several characteristic features appear in the antecedents of this episode. There was no overt enmity between the persons concerned, but there was a history of suspicion of *eye-pass*. In addition to the dispute between the parents there was the 'suspicious' association between Amir and Mahadeo. It was difficult for Nasruddin, his brother and father to believe that Amir had no hand in the slur cast on Nasruddin on the eve of his marriage. Nasruddin's accusation of 'playing repres-enter', and Ishmael's accusation of 'playing power-man' verbalize their conviction that their cousin was *eye-passing* them.

The feature of the incident which is relevant here is that Ishmael, who was not involved in the rice-field incident, should have waited so long to intervene. That he should intervene was likely, since he was the elder brother, and when he did he took the lead in the attack. Several reasons could account for the delay. He may have needed time to think it over, to be sure that Amir's behaviour had in fact been an *eye-pass*. Amir himself believed that Ishmael was instigated by his father. Yet what is most significant in this context is the fact that the most effective check to Amir's behaviour was delivered, not in the remoteness of the rice-field, but in the dwelling-area. Ishmael hurled his abuse standing on the farther side of the trench, so that Amir and the whole neighbourhood could hear his defiance. Amir might ignore taunts in the rice-field, but he could hardly do so in the residential area without being 'shamed'.

Abusive epithets delivered in public are carefully chosen to 'shame' and humiliate the victim. The cuckolding of a man and the promiscuity of his wife are favourite subjects, for example: 'Chetram! Joe Singh ah live with you wife! You nah see, you auntie man? You just like Christmas blow-blow.[1] When she done with Joe Singh, she go take all de men in de estate.'

A variation on direct abuse is 'throwing hints' or 'throwing remarks' in the presence of a crowd which, without ostensibly referring to the opponent, are understood by the listeners to be oblique references to him.

Scandal-mongering is another mode of conducting *eye-pass* disputes. There are many expressions for scandal-mongering: *to bad-talk, to talk me name, to get me name in you mouth, to talk other people story*. The person

[1] A penny whistle.

who does this is usually called a *Judas*, and occasionally a *santipee* (i.e. centipede). 'Talking name' is *prima facie* evidence of *eye-pass* and is sufficient in itself to trigger off a quarrel.

Abuse and scandal-mongering are intended to bring the dispute to the attention of the public; assault serves the same purpose even more strikingly. The manner in which it is committed may almost be described as conventionalized. The intention to commit assault and the name of the prospective victim are announced aloud and repeated all the way to the victim's home. The assailant, armed with stick, axe, shovel, or cutlass, walks along the dam between the rows of houses, inquiring aloud for his opponent, even though he knows perfectly well where he is. He may explain that he has been *eye-passed* and utter a series of fierce threats. This sounds the alarm, and a crowd follows him to his opponent's home. There he attracts still more attention by hammering on the fence, gate or stairway, and shouting out, 'Hi! Come out! Let me murder you', or 'Me go kill you today; when me done with you is de rope for me!'

At this point friends and neighbours may intervene and persuade him to depart in peace. Usually this requires much sympathetic soothing and is never immediately accepted. Intervention is made doubly difficult because soon the threatened person too is on the war-path, brandishing his weapons and countering threat with threat.

The infrequency with which anyone is actually wounded in these fights is remarkable, for few enter a fray without one or several weapons. The observer is struck by the number of blows, aimed from a few feet away, which miss their target. One man rushes at another with a stick and hits with shattering force the ground by his opponent's feet. If the attack is made with a cutlass the flat of the blade is used. When someone is wounded, there is some doubt whether it should not be attributed to an accident in the confusion of the brawl rather than to intentional assault. In a few instances the assailant waved his cutlass with such gusto that he wounded his friends; in one instance he wounded himself. On several occasions persons attempting to stop the brawl have themselves received the badly aimed blows.

An *eye-pass* dispute originates between two persons and is usually confined to them. But, as has been shown, it is conducted before the public and therefore involves the relationships of the contenders to outsiders not concerned in the dispute. Because of their obligations towards or claims against one or other of the contenders, outsiders may feel compelled to take sides. Consequently a dispute which originated between two persons can develop into one between groups.

Certain categories of persons are more likely to become involved in a dispute than others but, unlike the institution of the feud, there is no relationship by virtue of which a person is obliged to take sides. People join a quarrel only after due consideration of their interests and the relationships to which they give weight. An examination of some of the ties on which alliances are based and the factors which influence decisions to take sides emphasizes further the socially regulated character of *eye-pass* disputes.

The first point to note is that there are informal prohibitions against outsiders entering a dispute. Overt sympathy with one side, even though it may be disinterested, is usually interpreted as an assertion of superiority. The person who attempts to mediate and pacify runs the risk of being attacked himself.

Example VII

Pardessie owned a small cake-shop. A fellow shop-keeper told him that Hassa Boy used to steal his empty bottles and sell them to other cake-shops. Pardessie saw six empties in Hassa Boy's yard and demanded their return. Hassa Boy admitted having 'borrowed' them, and returned four a few days later. But despite repeated requests he delayed returning the other two. (It may be added that a year ago Hassa Boy's father had given material evidence against Pardessie's brother in a management inquiry into the latter's conduct resulting in his eviction from the estate.)

One evening Pardessie joined a drinking party of a group of friends known as 'the shop-keepers' because the main figures of this group were the two brothers who owned the local grocery and the owners of the two local cake-shops, Pardessie and Jacob Singh. After the party, Pardessie, Jacob Singh, his brother and two others were squatting on the dam when Hassa Boy passed by. One of them invited him for a drink. Hassa Boy did not see a bottle, so he said, 'Me nah see any rum; but if you want me for gaff, me go gaff with you.' Then Pardessie said, 'You is a damned f—— s——; me going beat you f—— rass.' Hassa Boy ran home and locked his door, pursued by Pardessie. Pardessie called him out, but he did not answer. Pardessie then taunted him. 'You rass, you dere with you daughter!' Hassa Boy refused to be provoked and replied, 'Man, if me tell you something you get me in worries.' Pardessie seized a stick and hammered at the gate, shouting out, 'Let him come out; let we beat him.'

Hassa Boy's wife appealed for help to their neighbour, Balwant, who came out and addressed Pardessie, 'Man you do wrong . . .', etc. Pardessie asked Balwant why he was so hostile, and why he was meddling in other people's affairs. Balwant replied that he was neither hostile nor meddling. Pardessie warned him of the dire consequences of 'playing representer'.

Balwant decided to call the police. On his way he passed Pardessie's companions and called out their names in order, so he explained, to remind them that they would be called as witnesses. Jacob Singh protested, 'Man, why you call out me name?' Balwant did not reply. On his way back Jacob again asked him why he called out his name. Balwant explained. Jacob replied that he did not like his name being called out like that and threatened to beat Balwant who defied him. A fight between them ensued.

Pardessie's willingness to precipitate a fight over two empties was not because he had suffered by their loss but because Hassa Boy riled him by ignoring his demand. Very probably Hassa Boy's offence was aggravated by his father's action in volunteering evidence against Pardessie's brother. Thus the quarrel arose not from a claim to superior prestige by Hassa Boy, but from an attempt by Pardessie to establish his superiority unequivocally. For Hassa Boy did not contest the fact of his inferior prestige. Pardessie's taunt of incest—'You dere with you daughter'—did not provoke him to aggression. Nor was this due to his peaceful disposition, since he showed no unwillingness to quarrel with other unskilled labourers like himself. Balwant had claims to a prestige comparable to that of the shop-keepers. He was not employed on the plantation but worked as a goldsmith, mechanic, and a 'dentist'. At one time he had been a taxi driver, and had captained the local cricket eleven. Pardessie, Jacob Singh, and Balwant, all felt entitled to prestige at a level at which competition was possible.

Balwant stated that he intervened because Pardessie's action was 'advantage pon Hassa Boy', and, as a neighbour, he felt called upon to oppose an unjust exercise of power. It may be added that there was a history of 'old spite' between Balwant and Pardessie because four years before Balwant had run away with Pardessie's wife, as a result of which there had been a fight between them leading to a case in court. In discussing the present fight Balwant criticized the shop-keepers who thought they were the 'big shots' of the area. Consequently, while it was possible that he had acted from altruistic motives, it is also likely that he welcomed an opportunity to demonstrate his superiority to Pardessie, if not to the others.

In this example, as in several others, intervention is in itself an *eye-pass*. According to the convention of disputing, outsiders may intervene to hold back someone who offers violence, but they cannot presume to judge the rights and wrongs of the case, which is what Balwant did. Pardessie was quick to infer Balwant's intention to assert his superiority ('play representer'). It will be remembered that in Example VI Amir's attempt to judge the issue provoked the accusation of 'power-man', and precipitated another quarrel. Jacob Singh interpreted Balwant's action as an *eye-pass* of them all, and his 'Man, why you call out me name?' signified his disapproval of Balwant's gratuitous interference. The attempt of an equal to act as arbitrator triggered off an entirely new quarrel. The right to stop quarrels, to arbitrate and apportion the blame, is seen as the business of superior authorities—the magistrate or the manager. Labourers are regarded as lacking authority or power to assume these functions. They may not, therefore, presume to judge their fellows—hence such accusations as *playing manager*, *playing magistrate*, *playing representer* and *playing power-man*.

The accusation of *eye-pass* thus acts as a sanction against the participation of outsiders in a dispute, even if they are bound by close ties to one of the disputants and are convinced of the justice of his cause. Friends seldom openly espouse one another's causes when the dispute comes out into the open. They may do so in subsequent discussions, and even offer to give evidence in a court case; but by then the open quarrel has subsided. The process of litigation represents a new and higher stage at which, it is recognized, other factors and norms come into play. Much less hostility is directed towards an unfavourable witness than towards an opponent's supporter in a quarrel. Recognized conventions thus serve to prevent disputes between individuals from becoming a general riot owing to the intervention of interested parties.

Close kin tend to be less restrained by these prohibitions, but there is no regularity in alignments which enables one to say that certain categories of kin will always take one another's side in a dispute. The factors that govern a kinsman's decision are many. Aspirations to a higher status and prestige, religious affiliation, economic interest and friendship weaken the solidarity of the kin group. The following example illustrates some of the considerations that can influence the decision to intervene:

Example VIII

Hassan and his wife, Fatima, quarrelled and separated, Fatima returned to her parents who lived in the same residential area. Hassan was befriended by the Imam,[1] a relative, who provided him with board and lodging. The Imam also attempted to 'reform' Hassan by persuading him to give up drinking, start to save, and attend the mosque regularly.

Fatima brought a suit for maintenance of children against Hassan and was awarded $4.00 per week. Hassan paid this sum until he quarrelled with Fatima's father and brothers over being refused access to his children. He insisted that he was paying for them but they told him he had no business to enter their house. Whereupon Hassan refused to pay maintenance.

After a few weeks Fatima sued him for $52.00 arrears. When he received the summons Hassan went to Fatima's parents and demanded the return of his children, because he was not going to pay any maintenance. This was refused.

A few hours later he reappeared on the further side of the canal outside his father-in-law's house. He waved the summons in the air and challenged them all to come out for he intended to beat them. Bottle Boy, one of Fatima's brothers, rushed out to the gate with a stick and answered Hassan threat for threat. He was followed by his father, his brothers, and his wife. The Imam came up to pacify Hassan. Fatima's family ignored the Imam and continued to threaten Hassan, but Bottle Boy's wife transferred her attentions to the Imam with 'You beard-man[2] rass! You rass ah uphold Hassan. Me go ah manager for all you. You ah play Judas!' Hassan rushed back into the Imam's house to fetch a cutlass, but the Imam's wife persuaded him to remain inside. Bottle Boy and his brothers continued to parade the dam with sticks and cutlasses and to fling taunts at Hassan until they were arrested by a constable.

The dispute was, strictly speaking, between Hassan on the one side and Fatima and her parents on the other. It is not surprising that Bottle Boy should participate in the clash, for he himself some weeks earlier had quarrelled with his parents and brothers and had only recently become reconciled. His conspicuous aggression in this dispute may be interpreted as an attempt to reaffirm his solidarity with his family. Bottle Boy's wife,

---

[1] Muslim priest.
[2] Imams usually wear beards; most other Indians have clean-shaven chins.

whose unpopularity with his family had caused the earlier quarrel, showed great enthusiasm in their cause by including the Imam in her invective, something the others did not do. On the day of the incident, and on the next, she continued the quarrel by 'throwing hints' at the Imam's wife. She withdrew from the dispute when her mother rebuked her for involving herself in a quarrel that did not concern her.

The behaviour of two other persons deserves comment. When the Imam was attacked, he did not reply, although, as he told me, he was tempted to do so. But he prayed to God for help and controlled his temper. He could not defend himself in the customary manner because, as a priest, a higher standard of ethics was expected of him. His prestige would have suffered more from participation than from neutrality. He had been recently appointed to the post, and had not yet gained the active support of the community. Though he may have been open to the charge of having instigated Hassan, he clearly preferred to behave in a manner appropriate to a priest rather than to defend himself.

The other person whose behaviour is of some interest is that of one of Fatima's brothers who lived two doors away from his father and watched the proceedings from his window. Unlike his brothers he gave no indication of being concerned in the dispute. His brothers were cane-cutters but he was a skilled labourer in the factory; the others were orthodox Muslims whereas he was a reformist Ahmediya. He took a highly critical view of his brothers' behaviour in this and other disputes, and considered that they behaved in a disorderly fashion because they lacked 'culture'.

SOCIAL STATUS AND DISPUTES

Disputes occur between persons of comparable prestige. A person whose superior prestige is assured is under no compulsion to defend himself when provoked and usually chooses to remain silent and aloof. There are few disputes between unskilled and skilled labourers, and practically none between Junior Staff and unskilled labourers. Even when actually challenged by an unskilled labourer, members of the Junior Staff are secure enough in the prestige of their status to treat such claims to parity as spurious. The following example illustrates such a case:

Example IX

Raghubir, a clerk, and Mohan Ram, a skilled electrician, were married to two sisters. Mohan Ram's prestige was higher than that of an ordinary skilled labourer because he had some secondary education, and his father was a shop-keeper.

Mohan Ram's wife quarrelled with him, left his house and went to live with her sister. Mohan Ram made several attempts to persuade her to return but she refused. He began to suspect Raghubir of encouraging her to refuse and nursed a strong resentment against him. He was responsible for the rumour that Raghubir was 'keeping' both sisters. In time the following clash between them occurred. (Account from police records.)

Raghubir made the following statement: 'I am a clerk at the . . . Office. Mohan Ram came to the counter and asked the counter clerk to make out a launch pass for him. . . . Mohan Ram further disclosed that the Assistant Accountant told him that he may obtain a pass from the counter clerk. Upon hearing this I told the counter clerk that he must not issue a pass unless it was authorized by the Sectional Manager. Although Mohan Ram was told by me that he could not get a pass, yet he insisted on the counter clerk writing out the pass and sending it to the Administrative Manager for his signature. Simultaneously I went to the Administrative Manager and told him what happened, and the result was that he cancelled the pass which was written by the counter clerk. When Mohan Ram learned that the pass had been cancelled he became highly indignant and shouted out, "You play one thing of youself. You flying too fast and you will drop fast. If I meet you outside I will kick you backside." This noise attracted the attention of the office personnel who ceased to work. Some of them who were unable to bear the noise were compelled to leave their desks. The counter clerk told Mohan Ram to stop making the noise but the latter still continued to do so. When he heard me telephoning for the police he jumped on his bicycle and rode away.'

The counter clerk stated: ' . . . Mohan Ram of . . . came to the office to ask for a pass for the launch. The Accountant instructed me to make out the pass for him. I made it and sent it for the Manager to sign. The Manager cancelled the pass, saying that Mohan Ram was forbidden to use the launch. Mohan Ram then accused Raghubir that it was he who caused him not to get a pass. He shouted loudly in the office saying, "You play one thing of youself. When birds have long heavy wings they does fly past their nests and drop down".'

Permits for the launch are easily obtainable for a variety of purposes. But Raghubir went out of his way to prevent Mohan Ram obtaining one, probably in retaliation for Mohan Ram's onslaughts on his reputation by 'talking his name'. To Mohan Ram, Raghubir's action intensified the supposed offence of 'keeping' his wife. The metaphor of the high-flying bird underlines the *eye-pass* basis of the dispute.

Raghubir did not answer Mohan Ram's fulminations, for, as a member of the Junior Staff, he could not indulge in obscene abuse or violent scenes in public which would have shown him to be 'common'. Polite language is a symbol of high status and in this example, as well as in Example VIII, persons of high status and aspirants to it refrained from adopting the customary mode of conducting disputes. Thus abuse and assault are characteristically low-status methods of disputing.

The Junior Staff is, as a whole, more adapted to values of individual achievement and resultant differences in prestige. They have no strong egalitarian sentiments and recognize occupational success by deference in other sectors of activity. Clerks are differentiated in the occupational structure in terms of posts obtained through seniority and/or merit. Competition for these positions takes place within the framework of the organization rather than through open quarrels.

6

Social Control—The Community

IN this chapter I discuss processes of social control within the plantation community in so far as they pertain to *eye-pass* offences. Social control may be analysed under two aspects: as socialization and as coercion. The first consists of processes which present the accepted values and norms of the group to its members, educate and encourage them to conform, and emphasize the dangers of non-conformity. Religion, education, and ceremonies of various kinds are, in this sense, social control. The second aspect consists of action which forces a member of the community not only to accept the norms but also to pay a penalty or make restitution for offending against them and to conform in future.

As socialization *eye-pass* disputes function effectively. Frequent quarrels, arising from a variety of situations, provide the assembled audience with concrete examples of acts which are within the norms of *mati* and those which are not. They issue a warning against the imprudence of claiming a superior prestige which cannot be clearly established. For in these controversies, in which each contender abuses and threatens the other in practically the same terms, neither gains a clear advantage. The resultant stalemate emphasizes the actual equivalence that prevails between the contenders. Furthermore, an offender's claim to superior prestige is, in structural terms, an attempt to dissociate himself from the community. But, in order to defend himself against counter-attack, he is compelled to appeal to this same community and thereby confirms his membership in it. The appeal to the public emphasizes the sense of community at the very moment when it appears to be called in question. Thus, by educating the public in the norms, urging conformity to them, and impressing on each member the model of society as an association of equals, *eye-pass* disputes act as effective controls of behaviour.

In its coercive aspect social control through *eye-pass* quarrels is not always effective. Fear of assault and shame at being abused can act as deterrents, but their coercive power is limited by the conventions of disputes. Weapons are not usually wielded in a manner calculated to do real harm and fighters can reasonably expect to be parted before the fight becomes serious. While people object to being abused they can defend themselves by hurling back the same epithets. Much of the abuse is stereotyped and does not in itself usually cause great embarrassment. Abuse is met with abuse, threats with threats, and blows with blows. The offender cannot be made to suffer a penalty or make restitution for this offence. If he is set on asserting his superiority he is likely to repeat his *eye-pass* in another context. In fact the dispute can intensify the competition between the contenders and, sometimes, marks the beginning of a prolonged exchange of hostile acts.

Nor is the public in a position to apply sanctions against the offender. The immediate concern is to stop the disturbance and no attempt is made to disentangle right from wrong, to ascertain guilt or apportion blame. It is only later that, through gossip, the facts are guessed at and scrutinized, but even then no clear picture emerges. People may express sympathies in subsequent discussions but no-one will act on them. Further, in the absence of any relevant organization, the public can apply sanctions only if there is general agreement, and this is absent in the usual type of dispute. An *eye-pass* is an offence against a particular individual and is not a sufficient basis for a communal reaction.

Even if the offender's guilt is clear no shame attaches to committing an *eye-pass*. While it is recognized as 'wrong' and evokes sporadic censure, nevertheless to get on in the world is one of the values of the wider society in which plantation workers live. The public is usually divided in its attitude to an offender because he observes the norms of *mati* in his relations with other persons and therefore his friends tend to sympathize with him. There is a widespread desire to increase one's own prestige, and a man's assertion of superiority can only upgrade those whom he is prepared to treat as his equals. The incentive to intervene and condemn is weakened still further by the fact that he will construe any move against him as 'playing power-man' or 'playing represener'. The upholder of the norm then finds himself accused of breaking it. Furthermore, disputes occur so frequently that long past but unforgotten quarrels are an element in the history of many relationships. The man who intervenes in a dispute by trying to decide on the rights and wrongs of the matter may find it very difficult to establish his status as a *bona fide* peacemaker not interested in fishing for prestige in troubled waters. However altruistic his motives, he is open to the accusation of being motivated by 'old spite'.

Yet, making a dispute public does stimulate processes of control, not during the quarrel but afterwards, and not by definition of the offence and the imposition of sanctions, but by mediation which aims at patching up the disagreement and restoring the *status quo*. This is not an inevitable sequel; whether it happens or not depends on several factors. In the first place, outsiders must feel that the breach is serious and could have disastrous consequences; friendly relations between the contenders must be important to someone who then feels that the dispute should be settled. The person most likely to be so concerned is one who stands in a close relation to both parties, such as a kinsman, a friend, or a neighbour. Common membership in a religious, labour, or sporting organization can also provide such a person. But he must be acceptable to both parties and his *bona fide* interest in mending the dispute must be beyond doubt. Priests and drivers, if they are sufficiently concerned, may play such a role.

The mediator resorts to persuasion rather than any form of coercion. A whole array of moral precepts and fables are brought into play. If he is confident of his position he may even point out to a contender, 'Man ah you do wrong'; but more usually he contents himself with stressing the need for harmony between the contenders as kinsmen, as neighbours, or even as Indians. Disputes controlled in this fashion are usually those between persons who belong to a closely knit group within the community, such as a kin group, a religious faction, or a clique of friends. If one or both contenders refuse to be reconciled, the mediator is helpless. He has no sanctions at his command and will not threaten the contenders or jeopardize his relationship with them in any way.

In some instances, when the general public considers itself affected by an individual's behaviour, an attempt is made to organize public opinion and bring pressure to bear on him to conform. This happens when the offender has *eye-passed* such a number of persons that his behaviour comes to be regarded as indicative of an attitude towards the whole community. The following example illustrates such a case:

Example X

Seonarine used to be an unskilled labourer and lived in the ranges. He fell ill and was declared medically unfit for manual labour. He started a little cake-shop with borrowed capital and people claim that they went out of their way to patronize it because he was a *mati* fallen on hard times.

When the Extra Nuclear Housing Scheme was started residents of the ranges built houses and shifted there. Seonarine too, now a relatively prosperous man, built a house in the Settlement.

The residents of the Settlement complain that his attitude to them has changed since he became prosperous and that he treats them in an off-hand manner. They criticize his 'ingratitude' for they feel it was they who built him up to what he is. A variety of stories about him are current, all of which illustrate his supposed attempts to alienate himself from the community.

It is said that before he built his new house he walked round the Settlement measuring all the houses, for he wished to build one bigger than that of anyone else. He is also supposed to have claimed that he had a 'bungalow type' house like the manager's, whereas the others had the ordinary 'coolie type'.

A neighbour's wife related how Seonarine's wife visited her, admired the fretwork decorations in her home, inquired who had made them and incorporated them in the new house, on a bigger scale. Another neighbour complained that he visited Seonarine when his house was completed to look around it. Seonarine's wife followed him up the stairs, sweeping away traces of mud and dust for, as he later learned from gossip, they did not want any 'dirty coolie feet' tramping up their stairs.

There was a more general complaint that Seonarine was increasingly dissociating himself from local activities, seldom accepting invitations, choosing his companions from relatively high-status persons in the neighbouring villages.

These numerous criticisms make it quite clear that the upwardly mobile Seonarine was leaving a wake of resentment behind him. It is significant that no-one had attempted to take up the issue in the customary manner. When I asked the man who complained about the stairs incident why he did not express his disapproval to Seonarine, he shrugged his shoulders and said, 'Wha' you go do?', i.e. nothing could be done about it. Seonarine was successfully establishing his superior prestige. He was moving up to the level of the more established shop-keepers and none of the lower-status labourers were in a position to challenge him on the grounds of *mati*. Those who had been *eye-passed* contented themselves with grumbling to each other, although the number of critics was sufficiently large to make Seonarine unpopular.

It is difficult to assess the degree of control which this sort of hostile public opinion can exercise. Certainly it seemed hardly to deter Seonarine. He reserved a little cubicle behind the counter for drivers and clerks when they came in for a drink, while labourers were accommodated on the outer side. It was rumoured that people were withdrawing their patronage from his shop (which was now a large grocery and hardware store) and that he was losing heavily. But this is doubtful; so far as I could observe, business at his shop appeared to be as brisk as that at any other.

Though sanctions cannot be readily exercised through activities such as commerce, the position of the public is stronger in other types of activities, such as ceremonies, in which, as the following example shows, public condemnation can make itself felt.

Example XI

More than twenty years ago Sharma, a mechanic in the factory, was dismissed by the factory manager. Shortly afterwards, at a Senior Staff Christmas party, this manager was shot dead. The police suspected Sharma who was arrested and charged with murder.

A long and famous trial followed. Local people believed that the factory manager had been shot by a fellow member of the Senior Staff. Sharma's arrest and trial were regarded as the victimization of a scapegoat, as still another sinister move to 'punish de coolie people dem'. The trial assumed symbolic proportions and became *l'affaire Dreyfus* of the Berbice Indians. The leading Indian lawyer of the county defended Sharma. It is said that several thousand dollars were collected by public subscription for trial expenses. Sharma was acquitted.

After his acquittal he enjoyed the prestige of a hero for a while. It is claimed that the money collected for his trial exceeded by far what was spent on his defence and, further, that he was helped with additional donations to start a new life. With this money he is supposed to have built a new house and set himself up in business as a contractor.

Now there is widespread complaint that he is 'playing braiga' on them all. He is said to be dissociating himself from all social contacts with ordinary labourers and no longer to welcome the visits of old friends. According to rumour he publicly upbraided his wife for chatting to 'common' people at the stand-pipe.

As a reaction to this, I was told, when his mother died, only relatives and friends from other areas joined in the mourning rites. Local residents stood outside on the dam and refrained from entering the house to participate in the ritual. However, everyone followed the coffin to the cemetery.

A funeral ceremony requires the voluntary participation of the local public. If the report is correct (I am inclined to regard it as somewhat exaggerated) the community refused to participate in the ceremony and make it a success befitting a man of his prestige and status. A full turn-out at a funeral or a wedding is a measure of the high esteem in which the organizer is held and establishes his reputation as a man of consequence in his community. Thus the public can cut a man down to size by boycotting his ceremonies.

The question is whether it was an effective sanction in Sharma's case; whether it could make him more conscientious in his demonstration of *mati* with the rest of the community. The fact that, when I took up residence there a year later, he was still unpopular and censured by public opinion suggests that the sanction was ineffective. All inquiries showed that Sharma was mainly interested in associating himself with a higher-status group which included the small business men, clerks, and teachers of the district. He had sent his sons to study abroad and was more concerned with politics at the county level than with community affairs. He had aligned himself at one time with an Indian rural middle-class opposition to the left-wing P.P.P. and this was, in the eyes of many labourers, an unforgivable betrayal.

Sharma had reached a plane at which he was no longer susceptible to local pressures. Ostracism, the only sanction the public can exercise, was not effective against a person who wished to dissociate himself from the local community.

Thus the achievement of a higher status, or realistic aspirations to it, lessens the effectiveness of control through public opinion. Both Seonarine and Sharma wished to dissociate themselves from the community of labourers. *Eye-pass* of their fellow residents was accompanied by a move into a higher-status group. Criticism of them was strong because their status was not yet established. But opposition was limited to criticism because they were in fact successfully freeing themselves from the bonds of *mati*. This is reflected in Sharma's views on the nature of the local community: that the Indians were backward, they did not like to see fellow Indians prosper, and made every effort to 'drag down' those who did.

The question arises whether a low-status labourer, who remains a full member of the community, can be controlled more effectively. I present below accounts of two disputes in which such persons had, or were judged to have, explicitly *eye-passed* the whole community. Communal reaction to these offences took the form of public meetings.

In the past meetings to discuss matters of common interest (other than labour disputes, discussion of which was forbidden) were held regularly. In recent times such meetings have been very rare, and it was a fortunate coincidence that two were held during my stay. Both meetings were called by the residents of one of the settlements of a plantation, where relative isolation has enhanced neighbourhood solidarity. This settlement has its own places of worship and religious associations distinct from those of the rest of the plantation. The meetings represent the utmost the community can do to control an individual's behaviour, and, though they are atypical forms of behaviour, they enable one to observe social processes which are prevalent, but less manifest, in the rest of the plantation. They throw some light on the effectiveness of public opinion and on the ability of the community to impose sanctions on its members.

Because these incidents involve several persons who are referred to by (fictitious) names, a list of the chief participants is given.

Example XII

Harry, donor of a wedding feast
Dyal, president, Hindu Church Committee } See *Example III*
Khan, president, Muslim Jamaat (orthodox)
Deen, secretary, Muslim Jamaat (orthodox)
Baldeo Singh, tractor-operator
Hercules, local rural constable
Hindu priest (pandit)
Muslim priest (Imam)

Harry was an unskilled labourer and a prominent member of the Jamaat. His eldest daughter was to be married shortly and he had invited the whole neighbourhood.

On several occasions during the fortnight before the wedding he had announced loudly that he would give all Hindu guests a 'bone to suck' and to all Muslim guests 'food for dogs'. Both these statements were calculated insults and were generally regarded as such. Still, there was no serious resentment. But he continued to repeat the insults on the night of the Sunday before the wedding, standing on a bridge and addressing the neighbourhood. The bridge is in a commanding position and his voice carried far.

Many were outraged. Deen and Khan, both unskilled labourers and office bearers in the Jamaat committee, began to mobilize public opinion against Harry. Their main arguments were that Harry had disgraced the Muslims and jeopardized Hindu-Muslim amity. They approached Dyal, who was president of the Hindu Church Committee, and requested the co-operation of the Hindus in a protest meeting at which Harry was to be asked for an explanation. The purpose of the meeting was to organize, if necessary, a boycott of Harry's daughter's wedding. Dyal readily assented and even canvassed Hindu support for taking some disciplinary action against Harry.

Before the meeting Dyal and Deen asked the pandit[1] to preside over it. They told him that the meeting should consider a boycott of the wedding. They stressed the necessity for informing Harry whether the people would attend the wedding or not so that he could prepare the feast accordingly. Dyal declared that this was doubly necessary lest Harry sue them in court for causing him unnecessary expense by accepting his invitation and not attending the wedding. Dyal also felt that, whether a boycott was imposed or not, the pandit should impose a fine of twenty-five dollars. The pandit agreed to preside at the meeting if he was assisted by the Imam as co-president; but he declined the responsibility for imposing a fine. He declared that the right to judge persons was the privilege of God; he would content himself with presiding over the meeting and leaving the rest to the people.

After Deen and Dyal left he remarked to me that if today he fined Harry, tomorrow everyone, including those who made the proposal, would turn against him for trying to assert his control over others and would try to oust him from office. He therefore proposed to have a 'jury' of six persons to decide the issue. He was so wary of exposing himself to any future criticism that, when I pointed out that in the event of a tie he would have the casting vote, he opted for a 'jury' of five or seven.

The meeting was held three days before the wedding in an open space by the settlement. Harry was conversing with others present and there was no visible constraint in their attitude to him. He was willing to discuss his offence freely and explained that he had 'bad-talked de people' when he was drunk.

The meeting turned out to be somewhat different from what the pandit expected. The audience gathered in a circle around him, Dyal, Deen, Khan, and Harry. The pandit opened the meeting by saying that they were assembled there to discuss a very serious matter. He could not proceed further for, while he was trying to silence the noisy assembly, Khan took over the meeting.

Khan outlined Harry's offence and told him how severely the community disapproved of it. Harry replied that he wished to apologize sincerely to everybody, that he had been drunk on Sunday night and wished to beg everyone's pardon.

Dyal interrupted him to say that this was not the correct procedure; witnesses should be called so that everyone could hear for himself the evidence against Harry. Two witnesses testified that they heard Harry make the alleged remarks. Harry was asked to 'cross-examine' them, which he did. Then Hercules, the local rural constable, was called on to testify. But Harry and a few others objected that this was an 'Indian business' and therefore it was 'out of order' for a Negro to testify. The debate over this point took some time. Eventually Khan declared, the rest concurring, that Hercules could testify because he had lived for so many years among them that he was thoroughly conversant with Indian customs; therefore, 'though he Black, he almost Indian' and could properly testify. Hercules too stated that he had heard Harry make the alleged remarks on various occasions.

Khan, summing up the case, stated that Harry had indeed committed a serious *eye-pass* of the people. Dyal suggested that the meeting come to some

[1] Hindu priest.

decision on the question of a boycott so as to give Harry fair warning. Harry repeated his apology begging everyone to attend and added that he had planned a lavish feast which he wished them all to enjoy.

One person asked him what assurance they had that he would not insult them again after the wedding was over. Harry promised solemnly not to do that; if he did, they could do with him as they liked. Some were not satisfied and demanded a stronger assurance. Khan reminded the meeting that the decision to boycott the wedding lay with it. There was a short lull.

Then Baldeo Singh, a tractor-operator, asked what the meeting was about, who summoned it, and who had authority to pass sentence on and punish others 'like dem was magistrate'. This question caused a big uproar and led to a marked division of opinion as to who had the right to punish Harry. Deen and Dyal attempted to explain matters to him but he rejected their explanations and insisted that there was no-one there to tell him what to do. If he felt like going to the wedding he would go; he dared anyone to stop him. Several followed his lead and the uproar increased.

Another speaker stated that since many had already accepted the invitation they could not refuse now. Deen argued that three days was adequate notice. In the meantime the pandit and Dyal were explaining to those influenced by Baldeo Singh that the meeting was convened by the Hindu Church Committee in co-operation with the Jamaat.

The assembly dissolved into small arguing groups. Some were repeating the point that Harry had offended the community, some were insisting that it was difficult not to attend, and Harry was repeating his apology over and over again. Although everyone was arguing at the top of his voice the mood of the assembly was far from serious. There was much laughter and banter; ironical cheers greeted each speaker. Khan again asked the assembly what decision it had arrived at. But the assembly showed nothing but indecision and confusion.

Harry repeated his apology again; if his remarks had offended the community, he wished to withdraw them and beg everybody's pardon; he could do no more and therefore it was up to them to accept it and attend the wedding; but if they did not wish to do so, they could keep away for he could get on very well without them.

There were murmurs of protest. Khan warned Harry to be penitent and patient and not fling his apology in their faces. Harry reiterated what he said. Khan muttered an oath of digust and stormed out. Harry's wife called out to him, 'Let we go now; nah worry with 'um.' Many protested that Harry was going back on his apology. Harry left and the meeting broke up.

Many agreed that 'Harry rascal—him worthless', but no-one knew whether there would be a boycott or not. No-one had come to any decision and all seemed to prefer to 'wait and see'.

The wedding was held on Sunday with a reasonable attendance. However, most of the guests were from other parts of the plantation and from the groom's village. Only six of the ninety-four household heads in the settlement attended. Of these two were Harry's immediate neighbours, one was a driver, and one was an Ahmediya who did not belong to the Jamaat.

The ultimate result of the meeting was the imposition of a penalty. So far as the local group was concerned Harry gained no prestige from the

wedding. Yet the boycott was carried out only after a great deal of indecision and almost, as it were, by accident. It can be argued that Harry
brought the sanction upon himself by his last outburst.

The opinions of the assembly were completely divided on three important issues: (a) on the right of the meeting to penalize Harry, (b) on the
good faith of those who organized the meeting, and (c) on the penalty that
should be imposed. When Baldeo Singh questioned the right of the meeting
to 'play magistrate' or to tell him what to do, he raised a sore point for
no-one could publicly claim that right for himself or in the name of the
collectivity. The meeting could not exercise any authority without recognition of its legitimate power or of its accredited representatives.

In discussions before the meeting many were wondering whether the
boycott move was not engineered by those who harboured 'old spite'
against Harry. Some recalled a long-standing dispute between Deen and
Harry; others referred to Harry's successive challenges to Khan's leadership of the Jamaat; others recalled Harry's dispute with Dyal. Looking at
the meeting in this light several were prepared to see it as 'other people
story' with which they were reluctant to meddle. There were others who
contended that Harry had attended their weddings bringing presents; it
was their duty to help at and attend his wedding now. Some felt that since
Harry was drunk when he uttered the offending remarks he should not be
censured too severely.

Thus the meeting was not united about its powers or its aims. It was
divided not only in opinion but also by cliques of friends, religious factions,
and kin groups. If Harry had been a less arrogant and objectionable person
it is unlikely that the neighbourhood would have supported any sanction
more serious than demanding an apology. Even while the meeting was
going on some felt that Deen and Dyal were pressing him too far. The
chances of the boycott proposal being carried were slight.

But Harry defied the whole meeting. He alienated his friends and sym-
pathizers and goaded them to imposing a boycott. His barely concealed
arrogance undermined his case and united an otherwise divided assembly.
But even this unity could not achieve very much, for Harry could count
on the attendance of residents from other settlements who could not be
bound by decisions made by the people of this settlement. While some of
these felt that they should fall in with any decisions made by the residents
of this settlement, many others stated that they were not concerned with
Harry's troubles with his neighbours. Even though they agreed that Harry
did *eye-pass* his fellow residents they felt that their obligation to attend the
wedding was more important. Furthermore, Harry's wife had several
brothers in other settlements; four of them were influential both in the
plantation and in the neighbouring villages and their prestige and influence
could ensure a fair number of guests. For instance, one of them, a prominent Ahmediya, circulated a garbled version of the dispute: Deen and Khan
had engineered the boycott because Harry had rejected their advice not to

invite Ahmediya to the wedding. This made attendance at the wedding a duty which every Ahmediya felt bound to fulfil.

Public opposition to Harry did not last long. Shortly after the wedding his relations with the others were back to normal. He felt secure enough to tease them about the good feast they missed, a joke they were prepared to appreciate. There was even a feeling that he had been persecuted by Khan and Deen. At the Jamaat elections, held four months later, there was a swing of opinion in Harry's favour. The dissidents in the association rounded up enough supporters to oust Khan and Deen from the offices of president and secretary, posts they had held or controlled indirectly for three or four years. Harry was elected president. This event was closely connected with the next public dispute which was, in a sense, a sequel to the previous one.

Example XIII

Haniff
Deen, formerly his friend, now his opponent
Khan, Deen's friend
Ahmed, Khan's son by first marriage
Ishmael, Khan's son by present marriage ⎫
Amir, Khan's sister's son   ⎬ See *Example VI*
Harry, president, Muslim Jamaat (orthodox) ⎭
Dyal, president, Hindu Church Committee
Deonarine, Secretary, Hindu Church Committee
Muslim priest, Imam of the local mosque
Muslim priest, Imam of a neighbouring mosque
Hindu priest, pandit of the local Hindu church
Hyder Ali, farmer

Haniff was a prominent member of the local Jamaat. He and Deen were friends and co-operated in several undertakings. One night Haniff was leaving Deen's home. It was very dark and Deen lent Haniff a stick as a protection against dogs. A few days later Haniff told Deen that he had lost the stick and gave him another in compensation.

In the months that followed the good relations between Haniff and Deen began to deteriorate for several reasons. (a) Many members of the Jamaat were becoming dissatisfied with the Deen-Khan regime. It was said that during the years Deen and Khan had controlled the mosque they had appropriated its resources to their own use. They appointed a new Imam who soon showed he was not a willing tool and supported the dissidents. The latter were mainly younger men whom Deen and Khan accused of being heretical Ahmediya. Haniff, as an elder Muslim, supported Deen and Khan. But the annual meeting which elected Harry president also elected two of Haniff's sons to the committee. Haniff found himself taking a favourable attitude to the new regime. (b) Haniff had leased several acres of the Rosignol backlands from the Government. What he and his sons could not use they rented to friends and relatives for a nominal fee. Deen used to have the use of two such acres each year. This year, owing to the approaching marriage of one of his sons as well as the pressing need of one of his wife's relatives,

Haniff did not offer Deen the use of the two acres. (c) Haniff's wife's sister, a widow, lived in the settlement with her daughter. The girl fell in love with a clerk, a Hindu, and the couple wished to get married. The widow favoured the match which was, from the point of view of status and prestige, more advantageous than anything she or Haniff could have arranged. The clerk's father, a driver, also agreed to the marriage but stipulated that the girl should become a Hindu. The widow consented. Deen and Khan censured her for being a party to this 'betrayal' and got her expelled from the Jamaat. Haniff had not opposed them at the time, at least not in public. One of the first actions of the new Jamaat committee was to readmit the widow.

As a result of these events relations between Haniff and Deen were poised on the brink of hostility. This broke out at a Koran *shereef* given by Ahmed.

Ahmed was Khan's son by a previous marriage. He lived apart from his father and relations between them were somewhat strained because Ahmed disapproved of Khan's second wife and his half-brothers, Ishmael and Nasruddin. There was a rumour that Khan's wife was Deen's mistress and in consequence relations between Ahmed and Deen were strained too.

Deen was not present at Ahmed's Koran *shereef* but his sons were. They saw Haniff at the ceremony carrying a stick which they said belonged to their father. They informed Deen who hurried to the spot and claimed the stick. Haniff denied that it was the same stick that had been lent him and reminded Deen that he had been compensated. There was a fierce argument as to whether the stick that had been lent was black or brown. Eventually Ahmed asked Deen and his sons to leave because they were disturbing the ceremony. Deen left, saying aloud, 'Me thank God that He keep me away from such hogs.'

At a Jamaat meeting held shortly afterwards Haniff, supported by Harry and Ahmed, brought a charge against Deen for calling the Muslims of the settlement 'hogs' and so grievously insulting them. Deen was expelled from the Jamaat and, in addition, it was decided to 'put him out', i.e. to boycott all his ceremonies and not to invite him to any.

Harry, as president of the Jamaat, called on Dyal, president of the Hindu Church Committee, to ask the Hindus to join the Muslims in boycotting Deen. Dyal refused to accede to the request, adding that, as far as he knew, there were deep divisions within the Jamaat on the matter. Harry insisted that he was making an official request with the backing of his committee and that, in accordance with accepted practice, Dyal was obliged to comply in the interests of Hindu-Muslim concord. The pandit advised Dyal to hold a meeting to discuss the matter and he agreed.

Dyal was right when he pointed out that there was no unanimity among the Muslims about Deen's expulsion and boycott. Several Muslims had not attended the election meeting or the subsequent one. Deen's expulsion came as a surprise but his followers recovered from their initial confusion and re-grouped. Khan supported Deen to the hilt and broke off all connection with the Jamaat. Their supporters openly challenged the Jamaat committee's right to expel Deen and publicized Deen's defence: that he had been grossly mis-interpreted for he had used the term 'hogs' to refer to Haniff and his sons and not to all the Muslims of the settlement.

The meeting was held and from its inception was a stormy one. The pandit

and Dyal opened it by explaining its purpose. Their addresses were continually interrupted by dissenting voices. Quite early in the meeting the pandit
and Dyal lost control of the proceedings. It was the forceful personality of
Deonarine, the secretary of the Hindu Church Committee, which ensured
a semblance of order.

One speaker declared that the meeting should be one of Hindus only. He
was opposed by another who said that all meetings were open to both
Hindus and Muslims. Another declared that it was not true to say that
the Jamaat had expelled Deen; a clique within it had done so. There was
therefore no necessity for the Hindus to decide whether to accede to the
boycott proposal. Deonarine himself pointed out that at the last meeting both
Hindus and Muslims agreed to boycott Harry. He could not understand
how Harry could now approach them as president of the Jamaat. If the
Muslims had decided to readmit Harry unilaterally, without the consent of
the Hindus, that was their own business. As far as the Hindus were concerned
the decision still stood and they were not obliged to recognize him as president. Ahmed explained that Harry had paid the penalty of a boycott of his
wedding; he had expiated his offence and was therefore readmitted. Others
contradicted him and asserted that Harry had defied the community.
Ishmael reminded Ahmed that he himself had boycotted the wedding because Harry had been unrepentant. Ahmed replied that he not only attended
the wedding but had also helped to cook. Baldeo Singh, who had thrown the
previous meeting into confusion, butted in again with the jibe that everyone
was talking nonsense because the previous meeting had decided nothing, nor,
despite all the hot air, could anyone present decide to boycott anyone else.

Speakers then gradually returned to the subject of Deen's offence. One
declared that this concerned only Muslims; he could not see why Hindus
were embroiling themselves in 'other people story'. Another, following the
cue, questioned the propriety of Dyal's calling a meeting. Still another challenged Deen's right to refuse to attend; the meeting was like the court and
Deen should be compelled to attend. Deen's son stated that his father had
instructed him to apologize for his absence; he would gladly attend a meeting
of Hindus only and answer their questions but he would have nothing to do
with the Jamaat committee. A suggestion that the Hindus reassemble in
Deen's house was howled down. Chaos broke out as the meeting disintegrated
into small gesticulating groups.

The next day Amir, who was Harry's friend and Khan's kinsman, told
Harry that the Muslims of the settlement were rapidly becoming the laughing-
stock of the district. He suggested a compromise: Harry was to withdraw
the decision expelling Deen, and Deen would apologize to the Jamaat. Harry
promised to discuss the proposal with the committee.

Amir then approached the Imam of a neighbouring mosque and another
respected Muslim of the district, Hyder Ali, who was also Haniff's sister's
husband. They agreed to intervene to settle the dispute. However, Amir did
not inform the Jamaat of this move; instead, he invited all the settlement
Muslims to a Koran *shereef*. Amir's invitation was acceptable to both factions
because of his close ties with both groups and also because he had remained
uncommitted during the dispute.

Before the Imam led the prayers at the ceremony Hyder Ali declared that,

CSGP H

much to his sorrow, he had heard that brotherly love no longer prevailed among the Muslims of the settlement. Before they invoked the peace and blessings of Allah it behoved them to feel nothing but amity and love. The Imam voiced similar opinions. Deen, Khan, Harry and Haniff agreed. Deen stated that if the Jamaat thought that he had referred to them as hogs, they were mistaken; if he had given the Jamaat any offence, he apologized. They all shook hands and the reading commenced.

This meeting, compared to the previous one, shows even less basic agreement or capacity to act in a concerted fashion. The community acted as separate groups differently oriented. The circumstances of the dispute brought to the fore several other disputes which obscured the main issue.

First, the Hindus did not think Deen's offence concerned them, while Harry's offence concerned a wedding, a ceremony which involves Hindus no less than Muslims. Hindu-Muslim differences are subordinate to communal interests, but improper behaviour at a Koran *shereef* and expulsion from the Jamaat are the concern of sub-groups. Personal factors intensified this divergence. In the first meeting close co-operation between the representatives of the two groups, Deen and Dyal, was possible; in the second the antagonism between the two representatives, Dyal and Harry, was an obstacle to any concerted action. Dyal refused to treat Harry's request with the consideration he would have shown had it come from Deen or Khan.

Second, the Muslims were far from unanimous. Khan placed his friendship with Deen above his loyalty to the Jamaat. Furthermore, in view of their close association in managing Jamaat affairs for several years, any censure of Deen would by implication include Khan. There was also the rift between the young liberals and the older conservatives, who were both seeking to influence the uncommitted majority. Although most members of the Jamaat supported Harry and the liberals and were pleased at Deen's eclipse, they were reluctant to go so far as to expel, still less to boycott him. By the time Khan came out openly for Deen many had begun to wonder whether Harry and the Jamaat committee had not gone too far in arrogating power. For instance, Amir felt that it was time the younger men controlled the Jamaat but he was opposed to Deen's expulsion. In his view the Jamaat committee was behaving 'as if dem was God' by usurping the right to exclude Muslims from religious activities.

Third, many reacted to the news of Deen's expulsion by harking back to his part in the meeting against Harry. There was a strong presumption that motives of revenge underlay the official charges. Consequently, again there was a reluctance to have any part in 'other people story'.

Fourth, Deen received powerful support from a group of consanguineally and affinally related households, which included twelve of the twenty-six Muslim households in the settlement. Not all of these households backed Deen—Ahmed, for instance, backed Harry, and Amir was uncommitted—but Deen had the active support of about seven of them and they led a counter-offensive against Harry's right to be president, rejected the authority of the new committee, claimed that Deen had been expelled at a poorly attended meeting, and were prepared for schism. They were numerous enough to compel the committee not to reject Amir's efforts to bring about a *rapprochement*.

The attempt to mobilize the public in order to penalize Deen brought to the surface a variety of other animosities between persons and groups. Harry, Haniff, Khan, and Deen held each other to a stalemate which threatened to disrupt the Jamaat. The dispute was settled by Amir's mediation. He was structurally well placed for undertaking this task. He belonged to the kin group which backed Deen but an earlier dispute with Khan and his sons prevented complete identification. He supported his friend Harry and the liberals at the elections but he was opposed to the expulsion. Thus he had close ties with each faction but was not completely identified with either. On the other hand he preferred to work behind the scenes and did not come forward openly as a mediator because he did not have the status to do so. He realized that there were grounds for suspecting his good faith and he moved cautiously lest he be accused of 'playing representer'.

Given the structure of the group involved in the dispute, the only persons who could effect a reconciliation were outsiders. Neither the Imam nor Hyder Ali could be suspected of asserting any superiority over the others because they did not belong to the settlement Jamaat. Besides, they were both persons of very high prestige, the one because of his office and the other because of his wealth and occupation. They were not potential competitors and therefore were well placed for acting as arbitrators. For although everyone knew that Allah had enjoined peace and brotherhood on them all, these two alone were in a position to draw attention to the norm. They did not enjoy any moral superiority: the Imam was facing votes of censure for alleged drunkenness in his own Jamaat, and it was rumoured that when Hyder Ali had been president of the same Jamaat he had appropriated its funds for his own use. Many settlement residents were aware of this.

Up to a point public opinion which manifested itself in these two meetings was an effective mechanism of social control. In the first meeting Harry attended his 'trial' and apologized for his behaviour. He recognized its authority and the effectiveness of its sanction. Deen did not attend his 'trial' but was careful to explain the reasons for his absence. He did not repudiate his obligation to attend and admitted the right of the public to condemn him. He was willing to apologize to the public but not to his personal enemies. The sanctions the public could exercise were powerful, for a boycott is a severe penalty. The decision to boycott Harry, even though made after the inconclusive meeting, resulted in only a small minority of the households of the neighbourhood attending the wedding.

On the other hand, it is obvious that in neither meeting was anything approaching unanimity attained. The numerous disputes between persons and between groups prevented the delegation to any one person or group of authority to impose the sanction. Although the sanction is a serious one the mechanism for exercising it is defective. Further, groups which are united on one issue are divided by other issues, so that the pattern of alignments changes with kaleidoscopic variety.

The organization of action for imposing sanctions requires leaders, but few persons have a record sufficiently clear of disputes to be in an unassailable position for mobilizing public opinion. Deen, Khan and Dyal had disputes with Harry and this effectively limited their ability to rally public support. Haniff and Harry were open to accusations, which were no doubt true, that they were using the Jamaat committee to work out their 'old spite' against Deen and Khan. The machinery for the co-operation of Hindus and Muslims was slowed down by the dispute between Dyal and Harry. Although Amir was strategically placed for undertaking the job of reconciliation he could not do it himself. It may be noted in passing that the very persons who are able to act as leaders have reached such positions only by leaving a long trail of disputes behind them.

In both meetings attempts to organize communal support for the exercise of sanctions were frustrated by the lack of recognized authority in any person, group or even in the community as a whole. When control was exercised, it was by persons outside the group. Since this dispute was couched in religious terms and waged within the religious organization, it was possible to find persons with the requisite influence because religion is the one activity at both local and district levels which is organized to produce such roles. But disputes between individuals can seldom be settled in this way. The person who wishes to obtain redress for an *eye-pass* offence has to depend on institutions located outside the social system of the local community.

EXTERNAL INSTITUTIONS OF SOCIAL CONTROL

In the recent past, when the manager exercised more power than he does today, his court was the institution on which the offended person relied for redress. It will be remembered that it was the policy of management to settle disputes between labourers, who were expected to bring their disputes to the manager before resorting to the magistrate's court. It appears that the police too brought offenders to the manager and would charge them only on his advice. Most disputes appear to have been settled in this way. The manager could penalize offenders and enforce his decisions because he could wield such effective sanctions as removal from one settlement of the plantation to another, suspension from work, and expulsion. But he usually tried to achieve a settlement satisfactory to all parties and exercised his sanctions only after repeated warnings. In its procedure, which allowed a great latitude in the admissibility of evidence, its interest in probing for the cause of the dispute, and its primary aim in restoring harmony, the manager's court resembled African tribal courts[1] rather than a modern court of law.

Complainants were allowed to file a suit in the magistrate's court only if the manager's advice, persuasion, and threats failed to produce a satisfactory solution, and then only with the manager's permission.

In most plantations the manager's court was held once a week or fortnight. A senior management official presided over it and recorded the verdicts together with brief notes on the disputants. Most of the cases brought before the manager's court were either marital and family disputes or *eye-pass* disputes.

During the post-war period changes in management policy, noted in Chapter 2, have led to a decreasing concern with the social life of the labourers. Assistant Personnel Managers have been appointed in most plantations and the settlement of labourers' disputes has been entrusted to their care. But today very few disputes are brought to the manager's court in Blairmont and these are redirected to the magistrate's court. There is no manager's court in Port Mourant.

The labourers themselves are becoming more conscious of their status as citizens whose rights are enforceable in courts of law. With the growth of trade unions and political parties, and the simultaneous rationalization and bureaucratization of management, there has been a decreasing reliance on the manager and even a reluctance to take complaints to him. The person who does so is apt to be dubbed a 'newscarrier'. The police and the magistrate's court have replaced the manager in the control and settlement of disputes among labourers.

[1] Epstein, 1958, Gluckman, 1955a.

7

Social Control—The Courts

ABUSE and assault, by which *eye-pass* disputes are usually conducted, are breaches of the law. In this chapter I examine the relation between disputes and courts.

The administration of justice in British Guiana is delegated to the Chief Justice's Department which supervises a hierarchy of courts and appoints magistrates and judges. This hierarchy consists of two tiers: Courts of Summary Jurisdiction (the Magistrates' Courts) and the Supreme Court. The Magistrate's Court deals with summary conviction offences and adjudicates on claims for debt and damages where the amount claimed does not exceed $250.00. It also makes preliminary inquiries into indictable offences and commits the accused, on *prima facie* evidence, for trial in the Supreme Court. Appeals lie from the Magistrate's Court to the Supreme Court whose decisions are final. Cases originating in the Supreme Court can be taken, on appeal, to the West Indian Court of Appeal and thence to the Privy Council.

This study is concerned only with the Magistrate's Court, because almost all legal actions in which local residents are involved originate and culminate in that Court.

THE MAGISTRATE'S COURT

The colony is divided into eight judicial districts in each of which there is usually one magistrate. Blairmont belongs to the judicial district of West Coast Berbice, and Port Mourant to that of Corentyne. Each district has several court-houses at which cases from the surrounding villages and plantations are heard. Cases from Blairmont are heard at the court-house in Blairmont, and those from Port Mourant at the court-house in Whim, a village about three miles away. The Blairmont court usually meets twice a month, with additional sittings if the volume of work requires them. The magistrate travels across from New Amsterdam. Whim has a resident magistrate; it is a much busier court which meets several times a week.

The court presents a scene of great bustle and activity. Sessions begin at nine in the morning, but a crowd gathers in the compound of the court-house an hour or more earlier. People wear their best formal dress, and their finery as well as the numerous vendors of sweets, drinks, and snacks give the scene a festive air. Litigants, usually accompanied by friends and relatives, arrive early, because lawyers conduct some of their business in the corridors of the court-house or in their cars, which are parked in the compound. Most lawyers are known by sight or by name. More experienced friends provide newcomers to the court with reviews of the available legal talent and estimates of costs.

In addition to litigants, their friends and relatives, several people are present because they have nothing else to do or because they like to follow court proceedings; these constitute, at a rough estimate, nearly a third of those present. One man explained that he liked to hear lawyers talk and gained much 'education' and 'ideas' in this manner. Another stated that he found the court as interesting as the cinema. More often than not the court-room is filled to capacity; there are people standing in the corridors and many more in the compound outside. Thus the proceedings of the court receive wide publicity. Within a few days, the verdict in a case involving local residents is circulated throughout the plantation.

Most lawyers in Berbice live in the town of New Amsterdam and tend to concentrate in one of its districts. Close interaction between lawyers in these 'circuits' has some bearing on the process of litigation. Their intimacy lends the court proceedings an air of informality. The division between contending litigants affects their respective counsel only formally, for amicable relations and co-operation between the lawyers cut across lawyer-client ties. The litigant, for his part, sees magistrate and lawyers as a group of outsiders characterized by education, power, and the habits and customs which express their superior status.

This view is enhanced by the ceremonial of the court which is entirely in the hands of the magistrate, the lawyers, and the police. The litigant has little influence over his fate at court: he is instructed when to speak, where he may stand, what he may say, and when he may leave. To many litigants the rules of the court are a body of esoteric lore which may be familiar but which they do not quite understand. They, as well as the audience, are sometimes reprimanded or ridiculed for improper actions, which serves to accentuate their status of laymen in a situation controlled by professional lawyers, the magistrate, and the police.

The lawyers and the magistrate can be classified as a group in terms of social status. By occupation, education, wealth, and a variety of cultural affinities, they belong to a high-status group. Most of these cultural affinities are the result of education in one of the few secondary schools in towns, training for the Bar in London, and membership of clubs in New Amsterdam and Georgetown. Ethnic differences—Negro, Indian, Chinese or Coloured—are insignificant compared to cultural and class uniformities. Behaviour in the court reflects social distinctions between bench and bar on the one hand, and litigants and audience on the other. One of the most striking differences lies in speech and modes of address. Distinctive terms such as 'My learned friend', 'My honourable colleague', 'Your Honour', 'Your Worship', etc., are used by members of the former group in addressing one another, but they do not use any such courtesy titles when address-ing litigants and witnesses, except on the rare occasion when someone of high status is involved. When lawyers speak to one another or to the magis-trate, they use what the labourers call 'high English', the educated Guianese variant of standard English. But they use the low-status dialect of *taki-taki* when speaking to litigants and witnesses. The transition from 'high English' to *taki-taki* is usually facile but quite marked. It is a clear indica-tion of whether a lawyer considers himself to be addressing an equal or an inferior. If a lawyer addresses a colleague in *taki-taki*, he commits a breach of court etiquette. A lawyer questions a witness in 'high English' to fluster him, or uses a 'correct' *taki-taki* to coax him.

Still, a certain familiarity is established between lawyers and labourers by repeated contact. The lawyer occupies a high and respected status in the labourer's social universe, and personal relations with him are highly valued. The labourer's contacts with persons of high status are usually in superordinate-subordinate relationships, as with management and Govern-ment officials. The lawyer, on the other hand, is not placed in any relation-ship of authority; he adopts an attitude of easy familiarity and is attentive to the labourer's complaints. It is one of the few relationships with persons of a higher status which give the labourer a more satisfying status than that of the ordinary 'coolie'.

Interest in lawyers is associated with considerable familiarity with the law and court procedure. Legal terminology has penetrated into the ordinary vocabulary. For instance, burglary is usually referred to as 'break and enter'; a man may explain that he 'go to court for disorderly'. When people quarrel, they act with an eye to collecting witnesses. The image of the Magistrate's Court guided behaviour in the public meetings described in the previous chapter.

People follow the performance of lawyers with great interest and discuss animatedly the merits of each case. They appreciate all the professional tricks of advocacy, and one of the star turns a lawyer can perform is to 'rough-up' a witness. This consists of glowering and shouting accusations like 'I put it to you that you are lying; you fabricated the whole story!' When this is done to an opponent, it affords a client considerable satis-faction. I was told by a lawyer how he lost a case and apologized to his client; the latter answered him, 'Nah worry, lawyer, you rough him up bad!' Big murder cases of the past assume a legendary character as those who attended the Supreme Court proceedings recount the high-lights of the trial and the tactics of nationally famous lawyers. Another topic of interest is the character of the magistrates, their partiality or impartiality, their severity or lenience, their alleged corruptibility or incorruptibility.

The police constitute the other important group in the court, the police prosecutions form a considerable part of its proceedings. The police are represented by a sergeant or an inspector, and two constables who act as court orderlies. The police tend to occupy a marginal position in relation to the group of lawyers and magistrates. Police constables live in barracks or in neighbouring villages, and by virtue of various relationships are, in a sense, members of the local community. But since they also belong to a national service and a hierarchy which is not a part of the plantation or village system, their membership is only partial.

The Police Station is an important institution of formal social control. The police listen to complaints. take statements, arrest offenders, and conduct other administrative duties. Because of its constant presence the Station exercises, in a sense, a more pervasive control than the court.

The police are assisted by rural constables who are local men. In plantations they are labourers nominated by management for the post. There are two rural constables in Blairmont and about four in Port Mourant. A rural constable is empowered to arrest a person and take him to the Station, where the police make out a charge based on his report. The rural constables, unlike the police constables, are full members of the local community and therefore their actions are not often seen as the operation of a supra-plantation official institution. Accusations of favouritism, corruption, and prejudice are frequently made, and it is alleged that giving them drinks and maintaining cordial relations is a wise insurance against future troubles.

THE COURT AND DISPUTES

The customary methods of controlling *eye-pass* offences are in themselves offences against the law. The courts and the police penalize abuse and assault by a series of legal actions, the commonest of which are charges of Assault, Abusive Language, Threatening Language, and Disorderly Behaviour. All these actions can be brought by the police; those relating to assault, threats, and abuse can also be brought by private persons.

In this section I shall consider the processes by which *eye-pass* disputes are, or are not, converted into court-cases, and their resolution, or failure to be resolved, in the court.

One of the most important means by which a dispute reaches the court is through police prosecution. This happens in two ways. One is a direct charge instituted by a policeman who is an eye-witness of the incident alleged to be a crime. In some cases the policeman warns the person or persons concerned that they are breaking the law, and if they persist he charges them. This procedure is so well known that many come to the police with a request that someone be warned.

The other way is through a complaint made at the Police Station. The police investigate the complaint and, if the evidence is sufficient, institute a charge. The complainant usually hopes that his opponent will be charged, but sometimes the investigation produces evidence that he too is guilty of the offence and then he himself is also charged. If the police are not satisfied that the complaint is based on sufficient evidence, they may refuse to prosecute and advise the complainant to institute private proceedings.

Such persons, as well as others who have not resorted to the police, retain a lawyer and instruct him to take action. A private action costs at least $5.00 in lawyer's fees, in addition to legal costs and inducements to witnesses, adding up to at least $10.00–15.00.[1]

Not all *eye-pass* disputes go up to the court. Except when a policeman himself makes a charge, the decision to prosecute lies with the disputants. Several factors may influence this decision, and these vary from one situation to another. Only a few of the more regular pressures which force disputes into court will be discussed here.

A dispute may be settled by the public duel if the offended person is satisfied that he has vindicated his prestige and proved the other no better than himself. The offender may be satisfied that he has shown himself to be unimpressed by the claims of the offended person, and has repudiated any suggestion that he should apologize, although he may feel that he has gone too far and may decide to be more circumspect in future. The hostility may persist for years, but there is a chance that, once the dispute has been made public, the intervention of mediators may settle the dispute to the satisfaction of both parties. In this case, the quarrel has had a cathartic effect: the tension has been released and the *status quo* has, formally, at least, been restored.

On the other hand, these results may not follow. One or both of the parties may consider that equilibrium has not been restored or the dispute so resolved as to satisfy the demands of prestige. No intermediary may be available, or his efforts may be unsuccessful. In these circumstances no satisfactory solution seems to be possible within the local social system. A person who does not wish to engage in public violence is also placed in the same position. The following episode illustrates some of these points.

Example XIV

On Phagwa night Seeram and his wife went to a friend's house for a chat; his two unmarried daughters remained at home. While he was away, three young men entered his house.

What happened there is uncertain. According to Seeram the young men molested the girls. Rumour had it that the girls flirted with the young men but, daunted by their boldness, cried out for help. There was a tussle between them. One of the boys apparently tried to drag one of the girls from the house, while her sister held her back.

Asraf Ali, a neighbour, tried to stop the young man, but soon he was wrestling with one of them. Seeram and his wife heard the cries and came running home, but the young men pushed them aside. Seeram claimed that one of the boys, as he departed, snatched a gold bangle from his wife's arm.

One of the young men lived with his elder brother, Biram Singh, a skilled labourer. The other two lived with their father, Sookwah, a driver's brother. Seeram complained to Biram Singh and to Sookwah, not directly, but through common friends. But neither Singh nor Sookwah approached him to say that he was sorry or offered to discipline the offenders.

[1] That is more than one week's wages of an average unskilled labourer.

Seeram considered this refusal to give him satisfaction as an *eye-pass*. As he saw it, both Singh and Sookwah, one because of his occupation, the other because of his brother, thought that they could *eye-pass* him, a mere field labourer, as they wished. However, he did not abuse or assault them, for he considered this to be 'bad behaviour'.

He laid a complaint at the Police Station, as a result of which the police charged the boys with assault. In addition, Seeram instituted his own actions against them, (*a*) for forcibly seizing the bangle (this was probably his fabrication), (*b*) for assaulting him, (*c*) for assaulting his wife. He claimed damages for (*b*) and (*c*).

According to Biram Singh, when his brother received the summons, he approached Seeram and asked him to drop the case, but Seeram answered, 'What me done, me done.' When I asked Singh whether he offered to apologize, he dismissed the suggestion and declared, 'Let him go to court, and he will see.'

The circumstances of the dispute were such that Seeram was compelled to go to court. For at least two ascertainable reasons he did not react in the normal fashion. One was his explicit reason that to indulge in abuse or assault was 'bad behaviour'. He was active in the reformist religious organization and aspired to be one of its leaders. He could not jeopardise his position of moral superiority vis-à-vis the mass of orthodox believers by behaving like anyone else. The other reason for his taking the matter to court was a strong rumour, of which he must have been aware, that his daughters had encouraged the boys and cried out for help only when they feared they would be 'caught'. The normal retaliation by abuse or violence would not disprove this aspersion on their reputation. Either he had to obtain an apology for Singh and Sookwah, or else take the matter to court in order to establish the boys' guilt and his daughters' innocence. Singh's and Sookwah's refusal to apologize left him with no alternative.

Singh made a half-hearted attempt to effect a settlement after his brother had received a summons. Bringing an action is in itself a sanction and many disputes are settled after the summons has been served, sometimes even after the parties have assembled in the yard outside the courthouse, waiting for the case to be called. In Examples VI and VII this occurred. In the first instance kinsmen of both parties had intervened to say, 'Boy, ah you make up you story and go home'; after some argument and persuasion they went away before their case was called. Similarly, in the second instance, a member of the Junior Staff who was a friend of both met them on their way to the court and persuaded them to 'make up the story'.

When a person brings an action the person who is sued soon hears about it. He has then to decide whether he wishes to settle or to continue with the dispute. Bringing an action in the same way as assault and abuse, makes the dispute public and indicates the intensity of the offended person's resentment. Similarly, like the public duel, it stimulates forces of reconciliation behind the scenes. An apology and payment of the cost of the summons is a common method of settling a dispute, at least temporarily.

There is widespread reluctance to give evidence in a court case, and a litigant, to be successful, needs to have sufficient influence to persuade others to testify for him. Kinsmen are not of much use as witnesses for lawyers will inevitably cite this link to devalue their testimony. Thus only a person of standing in the community, who can command the allegiance of others to testify for him, will readily embark on legal proceedings. In Example XIV Singh's willingness to let the dispute go to court reflected his confidence that Seeram did not control enough resources or persons to out-manoeuvre him. In fact, this was true for Seeram and the police both lost their cases. Although several neighbours could have testified on his behalf, only Asraf Ali was prepared to do so.

Winning a case and making one's opponent pay a fine, or at least costs, is thus an exhibition of power and an effective blow in the contest for prestige. As in the abusive duels, charges in court are met with cross-charges, and a defeat in one case is frequently an incentive for bringing another. The following example illustrates a complicated dispute with widespread repercussions in the courts.

Example XV

Khellawan and Jagdeo were neighbours. They quarrelled about a fence, each claiming it as his. One day Khellawan destroyed the fence and challenged Jagdeo to claim it. Jagdeo assaulted Khellawan who brought an action for assault against him. Jagdeo sued him for malicious damage to property. A common friend settled the matter, with the result that each dropped his case and Khellawan agreed to replace the fence. But he did not keep this part of the agreement. Jagdeo retaliated by 'throwing hints'. Khellawan countered by stoning Jagdeo's house several times. One day Jagdeo caught Khellawan and his son doing this and beat the son with a paling.

Three cases emerged from this incident: (*a*) the police, on Jagdeo's complaint, charged Khellawan and his son with 'throwing missiles'; (*b*) the police, on Khellawan's complaint, charged Jagdeo with assault; (*c*) Khellawan's son brought a private action against Jagdeo for assault and damages. Jagdeo was fined for assault, Khellawan and his son for 'throwing missiles', and Jagdeo was ordered to pay $40.00 damages. Jairam (a kinsman and neighbour) gave evidence for Khellawan in all three cases.

Hubert, Jagdeo's son-in-law who lived with him, met Jairam's daughter at the stand-pipe, called her a whore and stated publicly that he had slept with her. Jairam demanded satisfaction which Jagdeo and Hubert refused. Jairam brought an action against Hubert for abusive language (a charge of slander can be brought only in the Supreme Court), and Hubert was fined $7.50.

While this case was going on more missiles were thrown at Jagdeo's house. Hubert and Jagdeo's two sons went out and caught Jairam's and Khellawan's sons red-handed. A fight ensued in which one of Jagdeo's sons was injured. He brought a suit against Jairam's son, and was awarded $15.00 damages.

In the meantime Jairam himself did not feel that winning his case had sufficiently vindicated his daughter's honour. Even after the case Jagdeo and Hubert had not shown themselves in the least contrite. So Jairam let it be known that he intended to file an action for defamation in the Supreme Court against Hubert and Jagdeo, claiming $500.00 damages. The lawyer, he said, had asked for $100.00 as his initial fee. Jairam could not afford this himself and expected to receive contributions from his son-in-law and other relatives. He asserted that, because of Hubert's slander, he had found it impossible to secure a husband for his daughter. However, several other neighbours felt this to be a gross exaggeration.

Friends of Jairam and Jagdeo attempted to dissuade him from embarking on a Supreme Court case, but Jairam insisted that Jagdeo and Hubert would continue to 'bad-talk' him to the parents of prospective husbands. He had to show them 'me is who', i.e. that he was 'somebody'. But he also let it be known that he was willing to drop the case if he received an apology and the costs which he had already incurred. However, Jagdeo and Hubert refused to do this and said they were prepared to go to the Supreme Court.

I left the field shortly afterwards and have no information as to what followed. My impression is that Jairam was only threatening. Certainly the lawyer he mentioned knew nothing of such a client or such a case.

This example shows unusual pertinacity in litigation. Most labourers cannot afford such sustained legal action and call a halt at an earlier stage. In this instance all the parties concerned were relatively prosperous and could use lawyers and courts to further their disputes.

Such litigation reflects many elements present in most of the disputes taken to court. Bringing an action is an alternative to abuse and assault; sometimes both methods are employed. The harm suffered by the plaintiff, as defined by the legal action, is usually negligible. Further, by 'natural justice', when Khellawan stoned Jagdeo's house and Jagdeo assaulted him, the exchange was even. The incentive to resort to the court was the desire to get the other party fined. In the exercise of sanctions through the courts as many charges as possible are framed, if the resources allow it. A single fight can yield actions for threatening (or abusive) language, for assault, and for damages. Bringing an action is a hostile act which in some instances is met by assault or abuse (see Example VIII) and in others by cross-charges. The chief significance of a court case lies not so much in the fact that a particular act has been judged to be a punishable offence, as that the local community has been fully informed of the claims to prestige made by the contending parties and of the result of the contest. The magistrate's *ex cathedra* censures are particularly valuable in this context.

Bringing an action may be an intensification of a dispute. Jairam's threat to take his case to the Supreme Court was an expression of the seriousness of his resentment and a display of the power he was prepared to wield in his cause. Once an offended person's opponents and the public are convinced of his serious intentions, those with influence in the situation try to settle the dispute and vindicate his honour.

The court is the only institution readily available for the exercise of sanctions by one person against another. But to take a dispute to court costs time and money. Consequently, readiness to bring an action is the mark of a 'man of consequence' and in itself gives prestige. It indicates a person's ability to mobilize against his opponent the institutions of power of the wider society. It is a 'big-shot' way of dealing with a situation. A member of the Junior Staff does not descend to abuse and assault but gets the matter taken or takes it himself to court. 'Me beat you rass because me get money to pay lawyer' or '—to pay at court' (see Example V) are typical boasts.

This explains why the presence of a policeman has so little restraining influence on disorderly behaviour, as in Examples IV and V. In the former episode the disputants made such remarks as 'Who rass strong, let we beat *mati* and go to the Station', and 'When me done with all you, de Station dere for me', 'Then me tell him de Station dere for justice.' The policeman recorded 'Kausila said I must not talk to her; if I want let me carry them to the Station.' It can be argued that the conspicuous display of unlawful behaviour is also a method of attracting the attention of the police, in order to get the dispute taken out of the community to the court for judgment and punishment.

THE LAW AS SOCIAL CONTROL

Acts of violence produced by *eye-pass* disputes become the subject of court proceedings, but the court controls only the violence, not the dispute. The question it considers is whether the assault, abuse, or threats occurred in the manner alleged by the prosecution and whether these acts contravene the law. Usually this is not difficult to decide, for the law itself is framed in sufficiently general terms, so that a high degree of proof is not required. The matter on which the judicial process is focused is thus not central to the dispute.

Further, there is a tendency among accused persons to admit guilt in respect of the act with which they are charged, not because they are averse to lying (when the allegation is true), but because they are not concerned with that aspect. A common answer to the question 'Guilty or Not Guilty' is 'Guilty on Condition', by which the accused means that he is guilty in terms of the law but that, taking all factors into consideration, he could behave in no other fashion. But these factors are not relevant in the eyes of the law and can be admitted only in mitigation. In many cases, the accused did behave in the manner alleged. Consequently, many lawyers advise their clients to plead guilty and then plead for a lenient sentence. Each contestant pleads guilty and hopes that the magistrate will impose a heavier fine on the other. Pleading guilty is so much the normal practice that the dock is sometimes, and without irony, called the 'guilty-box', i.e. the place from which one pleads guilty. But this results in summary decisions. With greater experience of the law some are learning to plead 'not guilty' so as to get their cases heard at length, but for most labourers lack of resources limits their ability to embark on a long trial.

Little or no shame attaches to being convicted by the court of any of these offences. Friends sympathize with the man who is fined, and congratulate one who was acquitted or whose opponent was fined. A 'courtstory' is an experience many people expect to have several times in their lives.

Thus, in *eye-pass* disputes there appears to be a conflict of norms between the courts (representing the wider society) and the local community. The offence of *eye-pass* is not recognized in law and is seldom relevant as evidence. The acts that the court considers deviant and penalizes are special but recognized modes of behaviour in the community. The offence which caused the violence is not dealt with by court. Consequently, the same quarrel may reappear in several cases. In this sense, decisions of the court have little meaning as a solution of the dispute.

Some acts punished by the courts as infringements of social norms are not offences according to the standards of the community. In cases of abusive and threatening language, deviance and guilt hinge on the use of certain words and expressions, the provocative effect of which is inferred from their use. But this is not necessarily so, for such words and expressions are both current and acceptable among low-status groups. Their provocative effect can be postulated only if these words are taboo, as in the upper-status groups. However, among labourers, a father may say to his son, 'Bring dat rass shovel from de kitchen', or a grandmother may caution her grandson against jay-walking with: 'Hi, li'l boy! Get you rass ah road corner.' Such terms are so much part of the common idiom that sometimes it is arbitrary to make the danger to the public peace hang on the mere use of them. It can be argued that, if this danger were not already present, the obscene expressions could have no provocative effect. The cultural difference between one status group and another is such that what is an offence in one is not necessarily an offence in the other.

Again, an offence like disorderly behaviour is defined in an elastic and unspecified manner. A wide range of acts, not all necessarily disruptive of the peace, can be subsumed under it. For such conditions as 'in a public yard' or 'in a yard within public hearing' apply to almost every foot of space in a community which lives in closely packed rows of houses, and in which many activities take place in the open. There have been cases in which husband and wife, engaged in a private quarrel within their own home, have been charged with disorderly behaviour.

There is little censure within the community of offences punished by the court. Not to 'behave bad' is a mark of high status, and to 'get good behaviour' is an ethical ideal. But there is no condemnation of bad behaviour provided it is indulged in only occasionally and with good cause. Several rationalizations facilitate the inclusion of such acts within the range of permitted behaviour. They are regarded as actions expected of a man when he 'gets into a passion', which can happen to anyone if he does not have 'education' and 'culture'. Alternatively, such behaviour is dismissed as the result of intoxication. 'Is rum story', 'Is rum wha cause de trouble',

'Rum do you bad' are ready explanations of 'bad behaviour'. Other rationalizations are based on the inevitability of disputes and such local proverbs as 'teeth and tongue must bite' are cited. To 'behave bad' is thus, given the actor's low status, within the range of 'reasonable behaviour' to be expected of him.[1] There is therefore a discrepancy between the minimal norms of society and the kind of behaviour which is 'average' and permitted within the local community.

This does not mean, however, that the norms enforced by the court have no validity at the local level. Besides constituting a mark of high status, these norms perform another important function in the local community. While they are not the obligatory form of behaviour within the community, most of the cases arising from their breach are brought by members of the community themselves. The characteristic offences and disputes within the community arise from breaches of norms that are not enforceable in the court, and the local community has no effective means of controlling and resolving these disputes. They can, however, be subjected to the effective sanctions and control of the court if they are converted into offences against the norms of the wider society, i.e., into charges and acts of abuse and assault. The law is instrumental in this conversion. Quarrels are removed to the arena of the Magistrate's Court where bigger and better sticks are available for the prosecution of the dispute. Here each litigant vies with the other in using the court to demonstrate his own superiority and influence, his chief concern being that the court, which has the power he has not, should inflict effective sanctions for attacks on his prestige, a matter with which, of course, the court is not manifestly concerned. The lack of sources of power and authority within the community is remedied by this manipulation of the institutions of power and authority in the wider society.

In conclusion, it may be noted that, apart from its relations to management, the plantation community is not articulated with any other organizations of the wider society which have authority to regulate social behaviour. Plantations do not come under the jurisdiction of the District Commissioners, who administer only the villages, whereas the plantations are administered by management. The Administration of the Colony has control over plantations in a few matters, but this authority is still not freely exercised by officials who are reluctant to trespass on the manager's traditional preserve. The only organizations with the authority and power to regulate behaviour in the plantations—the court and the police—can be used only when an offence against the law has been committed. In some contexts at least it is paradoxical but true that the only way to maintain order is to break the law.

TYPES OF COURT CASES

In this section I present quantitative data on court cases and discuss the

[1] See the discussion of 'reasonable norms' and 'the reasonable man' in Gluckman, 1955a, chapter 3.

types of offences leading to them, their frequency, and their results. An examination of these data provides some confirmation of the analysis attempted in the preceding sections. In a sense, I shall be working backwards from the cases to the disputes and from the disputes to the social system. The difference in the types and frequencies of cases arising in villages and in plantations can be related to their respective social systems.

The analysis consists of a comparison of cases that come to the courts from the two plantations with those from two villages, one belonging to each area—Bush Lot, in West Coast Berbice, and Bush Lot, in Corentyne. Both these villages depend mainly on rice cultivation and very little on plantation labour. The population of both villages is almost totally Indian, and the vast majority are farmers working their own or rented land. For the limited purposes of this comparison, they may be regarded as representative of rice villages in Berbice, if not of the rest of British Guiana.[1]

Statistics of cases were obtained from the 'case-jackets' preserved at the Magistrate's Courts in New Amsterdam (for Blairmont and Bush Lot, W.C.B.) and in Whim (for Port Mourant and Bush Lot, Corentyne).[2] A case-jacket is the brief furnished to the magistrate for each case that comes before him, i.e. for each complaint filed at court. It gives the names and domicile of the accused/defendant and the prosecutor/plaintiff, and the subject of the case (Assault, Debt, etc.). The magistrate's decision is recorded on it. Information for Blairmont and Bush Lot, W.C.B., was collected for the years 1949–56 (inclusive); information for Port Mourant and Bush Lot, Corentyne, was collected for the years 1953–7 (inclusive). The records of cases for the years 1949–52 were not available at the Whim Court (they had presumably been destroyed). In the following comparisons I first compare the communities from the same district in order to make allowances for possible local differences between West Coast Berbice and Corentyne. An added reason for adopting this method is that figures tend to fluctuate from year to year and therefore it seems preferable to deal, initially at least, with figures for as many years as possible, i.e. eight years for the West Coast Berbice communities and five for the Corentyne communities. Once the general pattern of similarities and dissimilarities between the sets of figures has become clear, I proceed to a stricter comparison between all four communities for the four years 1953–6.

Blairmont and Bush Lot, West Coast Berbice

In the classification of cases in Tables I–IV (see Appendix), cases which arose out of similar acts have been grouped together, partly for convenience,

---

[1] For material on the social system of villages I have relied for the most part on researches conducted by Dr R. T. Smith in rice villages in West Coast Demerara. So far as I know, there is little difference between the villages of Berbice and Demerara in those aspects which are central to the comparisons made here, and with this Dr Smith is in agreement. See also Smith and Jayawardena, 1959.

[2] I wish to thank the Magistrates and Clerks of the Courts of New Amsterdam and Whim for permission to consult court records.

and partly because elaborate legal distinctions are irrelevant for this study. For instance, Common Assault and Assault Causing Actual Bodily Harm are grouped together as Assault; Larceny, Fraudulent Conversion, Unlawful Possession and Receiving are grouped under Larceny; Threatening Language, Threatening, Indecent Language, and Abusive Language are grouped under Provocative Language. A miscellany of offences arising from failure to have a licence for a particular activity (to drive a car, to distil rum, etc.) are grouped under Licences.

The first point to note is that the number of cases from each community is large:

	Population, 1956	Average number of cases per year (1949-56)
Blairmont	2,564	159
Bush Lot, West Coast Berbice	c. 3,500	147

The population figures are for one year only. Granting some imprecision, one can still say that, roughly, there is one court case for every 16 persons in Blairmont, and one for every 24 in Bush Lot, W.C.B. Estimating the adult population at approximately 40 per cent of the total, and recognizing that each case represents, on an average, at least two persons, one can say that in Blairmont, with an adult population of less than one thousand, about one in three persons is involved in a case each year. The frequency in Bush Lot, W.C.B., is less.

These ratios do not, of course, take into account the fact that local persons are sometimes involved in cases with people outside the local community. The following Table shows the number of cases in which an outsider is involved. Police prosecutions have been classified according to the position of the person on whose behalf the charge has been made—the 'virtual plaintiff' in the terminology of the courts. 'Internal' refers to all cases in which both parties are members of the local community; 'External' to cases where one party is an outsider; 'Government officials' are those civil servants (not the police) who prosecute for offences against sanitary or housing regulations, for failure to send children to school, to possess radio licences, etc.

TABLE 7

Territorial Distribution of Litigants:
Blairmont and Bush Lot, W.C.B., 1949–56

	Blairmont				Bush Lot, W.C.B.			
	Criminal		Civil		Criminal		Civil	
	Number	Per cent	Number	Per cent	Number	Per cent	Number	Per cent
External	15	1·7	76	19·7	11	2·0	114	18·7
Internal	786	88·4	308	80·3	504	95·4	495	81·3
Government	88	9·9	0	0	14	2·6	0	0
	889	100·0	384	100·0	529	100·0	609	100·0

The figures for the two communities are very similar. In both the number of criminal actions involving outsiders is very small. Since, as will be shown below, most of these cases arise from disputes involving some form of violence, one can conclude that disputes of this sort do not usually take place with persons outside the community. The proportion of civil cases with outsiders in both communities is much higher. This reflects the degree to which commercial dealings, such as purchases from stores, renting of rice-fields, tractors, and so on, extend across local boundaries. The people of Blairmont appear to contravene government regulations much more often than the people in Bush Lot, W.C.B.

One of the major differences between the two communities lies in the proportion of civil to criminal cases. The majority of cases from Bush Lot, W.C.B., appear as civil actions—609 out of 1,138 cases or 53·5 per cent. In Blairmont civil cases account for only 384 out of 1,273 cases or 30·2 per cent (Appendix, Tables I and II). The civil jurisdiction of the court is limited to cases concerning debt, damages, and recovery of chattels—all actions arising out of economic relations, with the exception of some actions for damages. The only important economic activity which is outside the jurisdiction of the court is the exercise of rights over land.

The considerably lower percentage of civil cases in Blairmont may be attributed to the fact that it is a community of labourers. In Bush Lot many cases arise from the accidental or wilful destruction of crops and fences, the network of mutual services in rice cultivation, loans and dealings with shops, rice-mills and tractor owners. But in Blairmont the primary economic relationship is with management and economic disputes appear as strikes and in proceedings of the Joint Committees. The comparatively fewer economic relations among labourers is seen more clearly in a more detailed examination of the percentages of civil cases. Rent, Hire, and Wages account for 3·9 per cent of the cases in Blairmont, but 11·0 per cent in Bush Lot, W.C.B. Actions for damages lie as a result of harm caused to both persons and property. It appears from observation in the courts that actions for damages from Blairmont were largely due to harm done to the person, whereas in Bush Lot, W.C.B., they were due to harm done to property, crops, and fences.

On the other hand, the proportion of criminal actions is 69·4 per cent in Blairmont and 45·2 per cent in Bush Lot, W.C.B. A detailed breakdown of these figures reveals significant differences, notably in the percentage of cases where some violence has been committed. The percentage of such cases in Blairmont (adding Assault, Provocative Language, and Disorderly Behaviour) is 40·0 per cent; in Bush Lot, W.C.B., 21·5 per cent. The reputation for 'bad behaviour' that plantation labourers have among villagers and the related opinion of villagers that they themselves are 'better behaved' seem to have some basis in fact. However, as will be shown, violence is only one method of disputing and a lower incidence of acts of violence does not necessarily mean greater harmony and co-operation.

Port Mourant and Bush Lot, Corentyne

A comparison between the two Corentyne communities (see Appendix, Tables III and IV) leads to the same conclusions as the comparison between the two West Coast Berbice communities. Port Mourant, with a population of about 9,272, has an average of 530 court cases a year, yielding a ratio of roughly one case per 17 persons. Bush Lot, Corentyne, with a population of about 1,680 has an average of 83 cases a year, yielding a ratio of approximately one case per 20 persons. Involvement in cases is thus somewhat higher in the plantation.[1]

The proportion of civil cases from the rice village (59·8 per cent) is higher than that for the plantation (29·8 per cent). Details indicate that this difference is very similar to that in the previous comparison: Rent, Hire, and Wages—3·1 per cent in Port Mourant, 10·6 per cent in Bush Lot, Corentyne; Damages—8·2 per cent in Port Mourant, 23·9 per cent in Bush Lot. The similar proportion for Debt (Port Mourant—15·3 per cent, Bush Lot—18·5 per cent) indicates a similar dependence on stores.

Differences in proportions of criminal actions are also comparable: Port Mourant—70·7 per cent, Bush Lot, Corentyne—40·2 per cent. The plantation again shows a much higher proportion of cases involving violence, 43·8 per cent as compared with 19·7 per cent for the village.

The Plantations and the Villages

The major differences between the kinds of cases from the plantations and the villages are summarized in the tables below, in which the cases are grouped under still wider categories. Traditional divisions of the law such as crime, tort, contract, and real property have been adopted with a few modifications, necessitated by the fact that a variety of acts are classified in law as crimes. A crime is usually defined as 'the subject matter of criminal proceedings', but failure to support a child, assaulting a neighbour, burgling a shop, attempting to commit suicide, and riding a bicycle without a light, are very different acts. It serves little purpose to group them together here.

For this reason criminal cases have been classified as Offences against the Public Order (including Assault, Disorderly Behaviour, Provocative Language, Vagrancy and Drunkenness); Offences against the Domestic Order (including Affiliation, Desertion and Maintenance, and Failure to educate a Child); Offences against Property (including Larceny, Injury to Property, and Criminal Trespass), and Miscellaneous Offences (including all other breaches of ordinances such as the Shop Acts, health and sanitary

---

[1] Owing to a series of copying errors I have been obliged to discard the information on the number of cases originating within these communities. My limited reading of the case-jackets suggests that the number of cases involving 'external' persons is slightly higher than in the two West Coast Berbice communities. This is a reflection of the greater degree of extra-community ties in this prosperous region of Corentyne.

regulations, traffic regulations, etc.). Attempted suicide has been placed in a separate category.

Civil cases have been classified as Liabilities in Tort (including Damages, Detinue, and Civil Trespass); Liabilities in Contract (including Rent, Hire, and Wages, Debt, Breach of Agreement, and Compensation), and Real Property (including Possession).

The classification preserves the broader legal distinctions with perhaps one exception. In the Laws of British Guiana, Assault is classed as an 'Offence against the Person' along with rape, seduction, etc., whereas Disorderly Behaviour and Abusive and Threatening Language are classified as 'Offences against the Public Order'. The classification of Assault as an Offence against the Public Order is justified in the present context for it is the sociological rather than the legal nature of the actions which is important in this study. Actions essentially the same are equally liable to be transmuted as actions for Assault or Abusive and Threatening Language depending on legal technicalities. If the evidence collected for an action for Assault is considered insufficient to prove the offence, the police or the lawyer will change the charge to one of Disorderly Behaviour or Abusive or Threatening Language. Judging by the customary modes of behaviour in such situations a person must necessarily have been abusive and disorderly before he committed an assault. Evidence collected to institute a charge of Assault is usually more than sufficient to sustain a charge of Disorderly Behaviour or Abusive Language.

TABLE 8

Frequency of Types of Cases, Blairmont and Bush Lot, W.C.B., 1949–56

Type of cases	Blairmont		Bush Lot, West Coast Berbice	
	Number	Per cent	Number	Per cent
Offences against the Public Order	519	40·8	247	21·7
Offences against the Domestic Order	149	11·7	45	4·0
Offences against Property	60	4·7	71	6·2
Attempted Suicide	2	0·2	0	0
Miscellaneous Offences	159	12·5	166	14·6
Real Property	15	1·2	6	0·5
Liabilities in Tort	97	7·6	212	18·6
Liabilities in Contract	272	21·3	391	34·4
Totals	1,273	100·0	1,138	100·0

Total $\chi^2 = 217\cdot7$; df 7; $p < \cdot001$

TABLE 9

Frequency of Types of Cases, Port Mourant and Bush Lot, Corentyne, 1953–7

Type of cases	Port Mourant		Bush Lot, Corentyne	
	Number	Per cent	Number	Per cent
Offences against the Public Order	1,174	44·3	82	19·8
Offences against the Domestic Order	265	10·0	18	4·3
Offences against Property	109	4·1	19	4·6
Attempted Suicide	6	0·2	0	0
Miscellaneous Offences	342	12·9	55	13·3
Real Property	25	0·9	7	1·7
Liabilities in Tort	238	9·0	108	26·0
Liabilities in Contract	493	18·6	126	30·3
Totals	2,652	100·0	415	100·0

Total $\chi^2 = 177·9$; df 7; p < ·001

TABLE 10

Frequency of Types of Cases, Blairmont and Port Mourant, 1953–6

Types of cases	Blairmont		Port Mourant	
	Number	Per cent	Number	Per cent
Offences against the Public Order	294	38·9	882	42·0
Offences against the Domestic Order	96	12·7	190	9·0
Offences against Property	22	2·9	80	3·8
Attempted Suicide	2	0·3	5	0·2
Miscellaneous Offences	96	12·7	291	13·8
Real Property	9	1·2	23	1·1
Liabilities in Tort	70	9·2	214	10·2
Liabilities in Contract	167	22·1	417	19·9
Totals	756	100·0	2,102	100·0

Total $\chi^2 = 12·4$; df 7; ·05 < p < ·10

TABLE II

Frequency of Types of Cases, Bush Lot, W.C.B. and Bush Lot, Corentyne, 1953–6

Types of cases	Bush Lot, West Coast Berbice		Bush Lot, Corentyne	
	Number	Per cent	Number	Per cent
Offences against the Public Order	145	22·4	62	19·9
Offences against the Domestic Order	33	5·1	17	5·4
Offences against Property	26	4·0	17	5·4
Attempted Suicide	0	0	0	0
Miscellaneous Offences	63	9·7	38	12·1
Real Property	5	0·8	6	1·9
Liabilities in Tort	119	18·4	80	25·6
Liabilities in Contract	257	39·6	93	29·7
Totals	648	100·0	313	100·0

Total $\chi^2 = 12\cdot7$; df 7; $\cdot05 < p < \cdot10$

Tables 8 and 9 illustrate the main differences between Blairmont and Bush Lot, W.C.B., and between Port Mourant and Bush Lot, Corentyne. There are relatively high proportions of offences against public order and relatively low proportions of cases in contract and tort in the two plantations, and relatively low proportions of offences against public order and relatively high proportions of cases in contract and tort in the two villages. The differences between each plantation and its corresponding village are statistically highly significant. Tables 10 and 11 show that there are minor differences between the two plantations and between the two villages but that these are of little significance.

COURT CASES AND SOCIAL SYSTEMS

The most important conclusions which may be drawn from the foregoing comparisons are: (a) the similarity between the plantations, (b) the similarity between the villages, and (c) the contrast and regularity of the differences between each plantation and its paired village. In this section I shall relate these differences to the social system of each type of community in order to emphasize the type of conflict characteristic of each. In this way the nature and functions of *eye-pass* disputes can be examined.

The proportions of cases arising out of real property rights are insignificant in both plantations and villages because most matters relating to rights over land are reserved for the Supreme Court. The number of cases that fall into the category 'miscellaneous offences' are similar in both types of community. There is also a similarity in the incidence of offences against property. The difference in the proportions of offences against domestic order is marked, but a discussion of this point is outside the scope of this study. The significant and relevant differences are, therefore, in the categories: offences against public order, liabilities in tort, and liabilities in contract. An examination of the proportions of cases in tort, which in the villages is double what it is in the plantations, will throw light on reasons for these differences.

An action in tort lies if a particular act infringes a legally recognized right of another in such a manner as to cause him some injury or loss. A man who is assaulted and injured can claim damages from his assailant, and a man whose crops are destroyed by trespassing cattle can claim damages from the owner of the cattle. Two classes of claims for damages may therefore be distinguished: those arising from injury to the person and those arising from injury or loss to property.

If the claims in villages arose from injury to the person one would expect a correspondingly high proportion of fights which would have been converted into one of the sub-types of the category of offences against public order, particularly Assault. But the relatively low frequency of cases in this category, and of Assault in particular (see Tables II and IV, Appendix), suggests that claims for damages are not a by-product of violence between persons, but rather arise from damage to property. The incidence of wilful damage to property, which is a crime, is very low in both villages and plantations. One can therefore conclude that the damage was due to negligence. The disputes reflected in these cases arise from the network of obligations entailed by various agricultural operations. Some of these disputes may also appear as cases in contract.

The plantations, with a much higher incidence of offences against public order, predicating a greater degree of personal violence, show a relatively lower incidence of claims for damages. This is not due to a lack of interest in claiming damages, for many rush to a doctor after a fight to obtain a medical certificate, even though the injuries are very slight. Rather is it due to the fact that injuries are relatively infrequent because of the stylized method of fighting. There are few reciprocal relations based on property and economic activities which can give rise to the kind of claims for damages found in the villages.

The central activities of the plantation community—cane cultivation, sugar production, wage-earning—are organized and controlled by management. Conflicts in these sectors take the form of dispute between labour and management. The labourers themselves are not bound to each other by reciprocal relations such that denial of reciprocity and the ability to cause each other loss can function as effective methods of exercising sanctions. With a relative lack of institutions through which disputes can be channelled and controlled, they tend to be expressed through quarrels involving violence.

In contrast, farming involves a complex system of rights and duties between members of the community: buying and selling, lending and borrowing, labour exchange at ploughing, sowing, harvesting, and threshing, renting tractors, oxen and carts, sharing water supplies and maintaining irrigation canals. A dispute between two farmers may be waged by one getting the other's cattle impounded for 'straying'. The common defence to a charge of letting cattle stray is that someone 'loosed' the cattle. This may or may not be true in any particular case, but the act is sufficiently familiar for it to be regarded as a good and ready-made defence. The man who is sued for trespass may in turn sue the other for breaching a dam and draining his field, thereby causing him loss.

Some of the cases arising from contractual liabilities also reflect such methods of exerting sanctions. The differences in cases in contract in the four communities (see Tables I–IV, Appendix) lie not in debt (which is mainly debt to shops and is similar in all four communities) but in Rent, Hire, and Wages, i.e. out of the reciprocal relations created by farming. Such cases are caused by allegations that an object hired or a job done has not been paid for, while the defence is that the rent had been paid or the job was a favour. In most such instances there is in the background a dispute of wider dimensions than the court case. For example, in a village near Blairmont, two farmers quarrelled over the conduct of a wedding and subsequently because they competed to buy the same piece of land. Each brought an action against the other: A sued B for damages caused to his field by B's cattle, while B denied that the cattle were his; B sued A for the hire of a tractor which A claimed was lent to him provided he filled the tank with petrol.

The extent to which bringing an action serves as a sanction can be gauged from an examination of the results of cases. This examination, based on the proportion of cases abandoned before they were submitted to the magistrate, provides an insight into the motives of litigants and the use they make of the court. I proceed on the assumption that many cases arise from disputes of wider dimensions than the issues debated in the court, which may or may not be central to the disputes. The litigant resorts to the court partly to obtain redress and partly to threaten his opponent and stimulate processes of mediation. If the second motive is predominant and bringing an action has been effective in this respect, a trial or hearing becomes superfluous. To be sure there are other factors which may lead to the withdrawal of a case, such as illness, high costs, pressure from lawyers, etc., but they are of marginal importance.

The figures discussed below relate only to Port Mourant and Bush Lot, Corentyne. The data on cases from Blairmont and Bush Lot, W.C.B., were collected during my first field trip when, unfortunately, I did not realize the significance of data on the results of cases. However, observation at court suggests that the results of cases from Blairmont and Bush Lot, W.C.B., would not be very different from those from Port Mourant and Bush Lot, Corentyne.

In Tables V–VIII (Appendix) court decisions have been grouped according to similarity of result. In criminal cases 'Order Made' refers to cases in which statutory duties (such as supporting children, etc.) are enforced; 'Committed' means committed for trial in the Supreme Court; 'Dismissed' means that the case has not been proved; 'Withdrawn' means that the plaintiff has withdrawn his case before trial (or in its early stages); 'N.A.P.S.O.' is an abbreviation for 'no appearance of parties—struck out'. In civil cases 'Judgment Awarded' means that the suit has been granted; 'Judgment by Consent' means that the contestants agreed that the magistrate should resolve the dispute without a detailed examination of the evidence; 'Settled' means almost the same as 'Withdrawn' except that the contestants inform the magistrate that they have composed their differences.

In the following tables I summarize the data presented in Tables V–VIII (Appendix) by combining the categories of results into two groups: cases submitted for adjudication and cases not submitted for adjudication. In the first group I include Order Made, Fined, Jailed, Committed, Reprimanded and Discharged, and Dismissed in criminal cases, and Judgment Awarded, Judgment by Consent, and Dismissed in civil cases. In the second group I include Withdrawn and N.A.P.S.O. in criminal cases and Withdrawn, Settled, and N.A.P.S.O. in civil cases. Cases are classified according to the categories already used.

TABLE 12

Results of Cases, Port Mourant, 1953–7

Type of cases	Cases submitted for adjudication		Cases not submitted for adjudication		Totals	
	Number	Per cent	Number	Per cent	Number	Per cent
Offences against the Public Order	598	50·9	576	49·1	1,174	100·0
Offences against the Domestic Order	109	41·1	156	58·9	265	100·0
Offences against Property	76	69·7	33	30·3	109	100·0
Attempted Suicide	6	100·0	0	0	6	100·0
Miscellaneous Offences	269	78·7	73	21·3	342	100·0
Real Property	7	28·0	18	72·0	25	100·0
Liabilities in Tort	79	33·2	159	66·8	238	100·0
Liabilities in Contract	282	57·2	211	42·8	493	100·0
Totals	1,426	53·8	1,226	46·2	2,652	100·0

Total $\chi^2 = 170\cdot6$; df 7; p < ·001

TABLE 13

Results of Cases, Bush Lot, Corentyne, 1953–7

Type of cases	Cases submitted for adjudication		Cases not submitted for adjudication		Totals	
	Number	Per cent	Number	Per cent	Number	Per cent
Offences against the Public Order	53	64·6	29	35·4	82	100·0
Offences against the Domestic Order	6	33·3	12	66·7	18	100·0
Offences against Property	13	68·4	6	31·6	19	100·0
Attempted Suicide	0	0	0	0	0	0
Miscellaneous Offences	43	78·2	12	21·8	55	100·0
Real Property	3	42·9	4	57·1	7	100·0
Liabilities in Tort	38	35·2	70	64·8	108	100·0
Liabilities in Contract	57	45·2	69	54·8	126	100·0
Totals	213	51·3	202	48·7	415	100·0

Total $\chi^2 = 41·0$; df 7; p < ·001

Two main points emerge from these tables. The first is the high proportion of cases not submitted for adjudication: 46·2 per cent in Port Mourant and 48·7 per cent in Bush Lot. The second is that the proportions of cases not submitted vary from one type of case to another. A high percentage of unsubmitted cases in any particular type suggests the use of legal proceedings to settle issues which are essentially outside the jurisdiction of the court. The disputes are resolved by threatening a rival and stimulating mediatory processes rather than by the adjudication of the magistrate.[1] If one regards the total percentages of cases not submitted (i.e. 46·2 per cent and 48·7 per cent) as the expected proportions in each type of case, then the degree to which the actual percentage in each type varies from that percentage indicates the extent to which the court has been used in this manner.

Examining the Port Mourant cases, with 46·2 per cent as the expected percentage, one finds that the greatest deviations below this figure are found in the types: attempted suicide, miscellaneous offences, and offences against property, of which the first two entirely and the last largely consist of prosecutions by the police and other government officials. One would not expect such persons to use court proceedings for the settlement of disputes outside the purview of the law. The greatest deviations above the

[1] Several cases of this kind are dismissed by the magistrate as trivial or unfounded. But the causes of dismissal are complex and it is preferable to exclude 'Dismissed' cases from an estimation of the degree to which the court is used in legally unrecognized disputes.

expected figures are found in the types: offences against domestic order, real property, and liabilities in tort. The first of these actions is almost entirely and the last two are entirely brought by private persons. I have discussed elsewhere the use of the court as a sanction in marital disputes.[1] Cases arising from real property rights are too few to be very significant. The use of actions for damages in *eye-pass* disputes has already been discussed.

In two types of cases the proportions of unsubmitted cases deviate only slightly from the expected percentage: offences against public order (49·1 per cent) and liabilities in contract (43·8 per cent). The lower than expected percentage of unsubmitted cases arising from contractual liabilities is probably due to the high proportion of debts to shops in this category. On the other hand, considering the nature and circumstances of *eye-pass* disputes, one would expect a higher percentage of unsubmitted cases in offences against public order.

The reason for this is that offences against public order include actions brought both by the police and by private persons. Four kinds of offences are included in this category: assault, disorderly behaviour, provocative language, and vagrancy and drunkenness. The police prosecute generally in the more serious breaches of the peace—assault and disorderly behaviour. Of these two they prefer the latter because it is easier to prove. They control offences involving provocative language rather by warning and advice. Private persons cannot bring an action for disorderly behaviour and assault is not easy to prove. Consequently actions alleging provocative language are the most popular among them.

In actions brought by the police only, i.e. disorderly behaviour and vagrancy and drunkenness (see Table V, Appendix), the percentages of unsubmitted cases are 20·2 and 18·2 respectively. In assault, which consists of actions brought both by police and by private persons, the percentage of unsubmitted cases is 42·8. In cases arising from provocative language, the 'people's action' *par excellence*, the percentage of unsubmitted cases is 69·4. These figures show that the degree to which criminal actions are used for disputes wider than the legal issue is what the preceding analysis leads one to expect.

The figures for Bush Lot are basically similar to those for Port Mourant. The greatest deviations below the expected percentage (48·7) appear in offences against property and in miscellaneous offences; there are no cases of attempted suicide. In contrast to the plantation a lower percentage in offences against public order suggests that the private use of criminal actions is not so extensive.[2]

---

[1] Jayawardena, 1960.

[2] The detailed percentages of unsubmitted cases are: assault—21·3, disorderly behaviour—4·6, provocative language—57·9; there are no cases of vagrancy and drunkenness. All these figures are lower than the corresponding figures for Port Mourant.

The highest proportions above the expected percentage are found in offences against domestic order and liabilities in tort. This is consonant with the statement that disputes in the villages are waged in terms of reciprocal rights and duties involved in farming. In contrast to Port Mourant, the proportion of unsubmitted cases in contractual liabilities is somewhat higher than the expected percentage, but less than might be expected if villagers used the courts as frequently as plantation labourers do. Thus it appears that the use of the court to wage or settle disputes is less in villages than in the plantations. In the following table the observed incidence of court cases from the two plantations and the two villages departs significantly from expected figures based on population figures and the assumption of uniform rates.

TABLE 14

Litigation Rates, Plantations and Villages, 1953–6

	Population	*Total no. of cases*	*No. of cases per* 100 *population*
Plantations	11,836	2,858	24
Villages	5,180	961	18

Total $\chi^2 = 49\cdot4$; df 1; p $< \cdot001$

Thus the parallel drawn between the modes of conducting disputes through the medium of the court, by means of criminal actions in the plantations and civil actions in the villages, should not be over-emphasized. For not only do villagers appear to use the court less, but it is difficult to decide to what extent court cases from villages reflect *eye-pass* disputes. Further, it appears that in villages disputes over prestige can be conducted by other means than violence and the court.

Smith states that in the village he studied there was an 'intense competition for prestige'.[1] This is true of the plantations too but, because of characteristics peculiar to each type of community, the competition entails different consequences. A community of farmers is more differentiated in terms of wealth, power, and prestige. Size of holdings and command over capital and labour resources vary,[2] resulting in marked differences in wealth. There is some control over internal affairs—through local government councils, irrigation boards, the Rice Producers' Association, etc.—which provides for a differential distribution of power. The achievement of appreciably varying degrees of power, wealth, and prestige is both feasible and recognized. Consequently norms are not mainly governed by an egalitarian ideology and a claim to superior prestige does not usually constitute an offence, i.e. an *eye-pass*. There is no comparable subordination to and conflict with a superior all-pervasive authority like management, serving to intensify group cohesion and sharpen the consciousness of being equal.

[1] Smith, 1957a, p. 28. See also Smith and Jayawardena, 1959, pp. 329–31.
[2] Smith, 1957b.

Smith points out that in the village in Demerara there were twenty-four associations and

... there are close on 300 offices to be filled in these various organizations. The proliferation of associational groupings, each with its hierarchy of offices, is one of the most interesting features of the life of this Indian community. Whilst it is true that the same individuals fill offices in several different associations, and that some of these associations are on the verge of collapse, there are still many positions to be filled by the adult males of the community.[1]

In addition to the acquisition of wealth, power, and the cultural symbols of high status, the holding of important positions in one or several of these associations is both an avenue for gaining prestige and an index of comparative achievement.

In the villages there is an institutional framework within which many disputes over prestige can be waged and resolved without recourse to violence or the court. The civil actions represent only one mode of disputing; since they are long and expensive, subject to much legal wrangling, postponements and manoeuvring with witnesses, civil actions are an appropriate medium for testing the relative wealth and influence of competitors for prestige. But conspicuous consumption and rivalry in elections to office in local and national organizations provide other modes.

In the plantations there is no such proliferation of associations, no such positions of prestige to channel competition and measure achievement. Claims to higher prestige cannot usually be substantiated by any real or marked achievement. Ideologically as well as in fact each person is the equal of every other in power. Rivals cannot be out-manoeuvred through institutions that regulate a mutually oriented activity in which one person can control the behaviour of another through denial of reciprocity. Both *eye-pass* offences and disorderly behaviour are characteristic features of the social system of the plantation.

In contrasting the nature of disputes in villages and plantations I have contrasted not absolute but relative tendencies, overstating my case slightly, perhaps, for the sake of clarity. *Eye-pass* is not unknown in villages and competition for prestige through office occurs in plantations, though to a limited extent. Breaches of the peace, as the figures indicate, are not uncommon in villages and disputes arising from denial of recognized obligations occur in plantations. It should be noted that a considerable portion of plantation labour is obtained from the villages and few villages are completely independent of work in the plantations. In several villages there are plantation labourers who do not depend to any great extent on rice cultivation. The social systems compared here are ideal types, whereas actual communities represent 'mixed' types. In so far as the types of conflict described are products of ideal systems, one finds both types of dispute in both types of community but with characteristically varying frequencies.

[1] Smith, 1957a, p. 13.

8

Conclusion

ONE of the aims of this study, as stated at the outset, has been to explore the validity of certain propositions about the nature and functions of social conflict, to see how far they can shed light on the working of the social system of the plantation. It is evident that I have found several of these propositions useful in the analysis of *eye-pass* disputes. In this chapter I attempt to make explicit the propositions which have been implicit in this study and to relate them to the disputes I have discussed.

THE STUDY OF SOCIAL CONFLICT

Coser points out that the study of conflict as an approach to the problem of 'how a social system works' is almost as old as sociology.[1] He cites Giddings, Cooley, Ross, Ward, and Veblen as sociologists who regarded conflict as an essential and central theme in the study of society; to them it was a basic form of social interaction. He suggests that, with the development of systematic sociology, conflict came to be regarded rather as deviant behaviour, a symptom of maladjustment which could (and should) be eliminated by restoring the social system to its original equilibrium. Conflict was equated with anomy. Dahrendorf has gone further to trace a shift from a 'coercion theory of society' to an 'integration theory of society'.[2]

In social anthropology, interest in such institutions as warfare, the feud, witchcraft, secret societies, and joking relationships[3] shows that anthropologists have traditionally taken a broader view of social integration than sociologists. In recent times there has been a marked trend toward a dynamic approach which attempts to include conflict and change as inevitable and essential aspects of the social process. Firth's concept of 'social organisation'[4] takes account of choice between conflicting interests, goals and norms. Leach presents the political system of the Kachins as being in a state of flux between two ideal and conflicting models, the social process being essentially one of choosing between rival modes of ordering social relations.[5] Fortes states that 'social relationships in Taleland fluctuate between amity and discord, co-operation and conflict, for forces engendering

[1] Coser, 1956, pp. 15–33.   [2] Dahrendorf, 1958a, 1958b, and 1959, chapter 5.
[3] See especially Wedgwood, 1930a, 1930b, Warner, 1931, Evans-Pritchard, 1937, Radcliffe-Brown, 1952, and Nadel, 1952.
[4] Firth, 1954, 1955.   [5] Leach, 1954.

both are always active; but in the long run an equilibrium is maintained'.[1]

It is as a special development of this trend that Gluckman's approach to the study of social conflict should be considered. The work of Coser, Dahrendorf, Bernard, Bendix, and the critics of the 'Human Relations School' in industrial sociology represents a parallel trend in sociology.

While agreeing that this new trend can provide further insight into the social process, it is not necessary to go so far as to regard it as a new kind of sociological analysis, as Dahrendorf does. He speaks of the 'two faces of society', drawing a radical distinction between an 'integration theory of society' (as exemplified by Parsons) and a 'coercion theory of society' (as exemplified by Marx). He states that these two approaches should not be regarded as mutually exclusive but as complementary. But he preserves the distinction in a methodological sense in order to study problems relating to conflict and change. According to him these problems require special analytical concepts because 'structural-functional' theory, based on concepts of stability, integration, functional co-ordination and consensus, cannot cope with problems of conflict and change. Consequently he advocates a model which is the diametrical opposite of this: that every society is unstable, riddled with conflict, in a state of disintegration, and held together by coercion.

A detailed application of his theory to empirical data is not necessary to reveal the inadequacies of this approach. Dahrendorf throws 'structural-functional' theory overboard because it cannot explain such problems as why a building workers' strike in Berlin in 1953 became a political revolt.[2] According to him this conflict produced dissensus and disintegration and can be better explained by his model of 'anomy'. But, by dispensing with the concept of functional differentiation and co-ordination, he is left without any means of distinguishing between the conflict of groups or quasi-groups in economic relations (classes, trade unions, etc.) and the conflict of groups or quasi-groups in political relations (parties, interest groups, etc.). At the same time he poses his problem in terms of such a functional differentiation by referring to the transformation of a *strike* into a *revolt*. Such a transformation cannot be explained without reference to a system of institutions functionally interrelated in such a manner that conflict in one can lead to conflict in another. The transformation of wage disputes into riots during the indenture period in British Guiana, for instance, was a consequence of the close interdependence of economic, political, and legal institutions.

It is difficult to conceive of conflict meaningfully without postulating a wider system of interaction within which it occurs. Nor can one conceive of the disruption and change caused by conflict unless one approaches these processes through the system that is being disrupted or changed. The model of an unstable, conflict-ridden and disintegrating society destroys the framework necessary for the location and evaluation of conflict

[1] Fortes, 1940, p. 271.   [2] Dahrendorf, 1958a.

and change. Further, it is generally recognized that such concepts as 'structure' and 'function' are assumptions made for purposes of analysis. They are points of departure that do not entail any conclusions about stability and consensus. These latter are now accepted as relative states and the degree to which they can be said to be present in a given system is a matter for empirical verification; they are not axioms.

The model of anomy is an inadequate approach to the study of conflict because there can be no systematic study of society unless one expects to find regularities and inter-connections, i.e. unless one approaches social facts as if their interrelations constituted a system. In this sense sociology is primarily concerned with integration; social change is no more than movement in a discernible direction toward reintegration. Dahrendorf's alternatives of an 'integration theory' or a 'coercion theory' as representing distinct though complementary approaches to the study of society are unsatisfactory because coercion is not 'complementary' to integration. Coercion is a mode of integration just as much as consensus. Whether it is a lasting or ethically desirable mode of integration is a different question.

The approach to the study of conflict adopted by Gluckman and Coser, which relates conflict to the concepts of 'social system' and 'function', is much more fruitful. It explicitly recognizes conflict as an inevitable consequence of the operation of a social system and raises the question whether, under certain conditions, it may not have a positive function, i.e. whether it may not contribute toward the maintenance of the system.

Such an approach, in effect, resolves the contradiction between two propositions: that conflicts are disruptive and that conflicts are inevitable. It poses the problem of how, given both propositions, a social system can persist as a 'going concern'.

Thus conflicts can be differentiated into those which arise 'within' a system and those that arise 'about' it. Coser distinguishes between conflicts which occur 'over basic matters of principle' and those which occur 'over matters presupposing adherence to the same principle'.[1] The latter type of conflict is not necessarily disruptive. A similar distinction is drawn by Simpson between 'non-communal' conflict, which is disruptive, and 'communal' conflict which is not necessarily so.[2] The same idea underlies Gluckman's distinction between a repetitive social system, resulting from conflicts resolvable within it, and a changing social system, resulting from conflicts that cannot be resolved without structural change.[3] He also distinguishes between revolution, which seeks to change the political structure, and rebellion, which aims at a rearrangement of personnel within it. He points out that feuds among the Nuer and struggles for the throne between Zulu princes occurred within social systems which contained these conflicts and were not disrupted by them.[4] Turner has shown how conflicts in Ndembu social structure are contained within a wider society

---

[1] Coser, op. cit., pp. 72–6; see also Coser, 1957. [2] Simpson, 1937.
[3] Gluckman, 1940. [4] Gluckman, 1955b, chapters 1 and 2.

which 'persists within the framework of the ritual cults'.[1] In all these cases conflict occurs within a basic consensus, a set of values and norms accepted by the contending parties.

The one difficulty with this proposition is that no criterion has been suggested for deciding when there is basic consensus and when there is none. If, in a democratic political system, one party aims at seizing power by force, is this consensus, in that all groups are still agreed on the importance of controlling the state, or lack of consensus, in that one party rejects constitutional means? Perhaps this dilemma can be resolved by defining carefully the particular span of the system one is dealing with. Thus what is lack of consensus within a given system could be consensus within a wider, more inclusive system or one defined in other terms.

Conflict not only need not disrupt a social system; it may contribute toward its maintenance. Coser emphasizes Simmel's thesis that conflict is a mode of interaction, i.e. it creates a relationship between persons and between groups. It does so in two senses. First by emphasizing danger to common interests it may unite diverse groups. Secondly it may integrate dissociated or inadequately integrated persons and groups. An example of this is Gluckman's analysis of a function of rebellion in the nineteenth-century Zulu political system in which, in the absence of a closely integrated economic and administrative system welding together the scattered units of the empire, struggles for the imperial throne inhibited separatist tendencies.[2] This, of course, is not an inevitable result but a tendency, for there are other conditions conducive to the integrative functions of conflict.

One of these is the multiplicity of conflicts within a social system which, Gluckman states, creates a 'division of society into a series of opposed groups with cross-cutting membership'.[3] Enemies in one situation of conflict are allies in another and the potentiality of conflict between allies inhibits alignments along one axis which may lead to a basic cleavage in the society. Coser too points out that social systems 'tend to be sewn together by multiple and multiform conflicts'.[4] He also suggests a differentiation between elastic and rigid social systems. The former type tolerates open and direct expression of conflict and allows for organizational adjustments resulting therefrom. The latter type, by suppressing all manifestation of conflict, 'exerts pressure towards the emergence of radical cleavages and violent forms of conflict' which result in the breakdown of the system.[5]

If conflict is 'permitted' in some social systems one can expect institutionalized arrangements for its expression. Socially regulated conflict has for long interested anthropologists. Duels, feuds, some types of warfare, witchcraft, and joking relationships can all be subsumed under this category. Analysing the rituals of rebellion in South-East Africa (among the Zulu and the Swazi), Gluckman interprets these ceremonial disputes as acting the fundamental conflicts of the social system.[6] The degree to which

[1] Turner, 1957, p. 330.   [2] Gluckman, 1955b.   [3] Gluckman, 1954a.
[4] Coser, 1956, p. 80.   [5] Coser, 1957.   [6] Gluckman, 1954b.

conflict is regulated can vary, but in all cases conflict tends to minimize its dysfunctions by channelling behaviour along controllable lines. Thus Frankenberg describes conflicts within the social system of a Welsh village as institutionalized in the activities of its football clubs, brass bands, and carnival associations. Disputes may wreck particular associations but they do not disrupt the overall harmony of the community which is reasserted through new associations.[1]

THE NATURE OF EYE-PASS DISPUTES

Eye-pass disputes occur with such frequency that, if one assumes that all conflict is essentially dysfunctional, the social system of the plantation must be regarded as an example of complete disintegration. But far from this being so, the analysis of this type of dispute, based on some of the propositions outlined in the preceding section, has indicated the usefulness of a broader view of conflict. In order to emphasize this point I recapitulate my argument briefly and, in doing so, define some incidental issues more clearly.

The plantation community is essentially a segment of Guianese society. The allocation of statuses, roles, and rewards within this segment is governed by norms formulated and enforced at the level of the total society. For this reason the wider social system has been the point of departure for the study of behaviour within its constituent unit.

Thus stratification within the plantation is an aspect of the stratification of the wider society. The unskilled labourers, with whom this study is mainly concerned, occupy a low status and are accorded little power both within the plantation and in the wider system. The value of individual attainments, the prestige of achievements and success, the competition for prestige, and motivations toward upward social mobility are important in the plantation because its residents are members of Guianese society.

The structure of Guianese society results in the creation of resident communities on plantations. These communities develop social processes and values of their own, which do not negate the processes and values of the wider system, but derive their force from the special conditions with which plantation labourers are faced.

So far as the study of *eye-pass* disputes is concerned, the most important factor produced by plantation social conditions is the egalitarian ideology of *mati*. It provides the norms for regulating key social relations. According to this ideology all plantation labourers (and, to a lesser degree, all plantation residents) are equal in status, prestige, and power. The notions that no-one is better than another, that what one person deserves all deserve, that one person's interests are the same as those of another are important norms.

---

[1] Frankenberg, 1957. He points out, nevertheless, that this is not an even, cyclical process. The break-up of one association prejudices the chances of survival of its successor, for disputes tend to be carried over and accumulated.

The relation of ideology to social structure is not a simple one. It is an interpretation of social structure but not necessarily a mirror of it. Parsons points out that in an ideology 'empirical elements are combined with and shade off into non-empirical elements at points where justification of the ultimate goals and values of collective action become involved'.[1] In the sense that an ideology selects and emphasizes certain roles, and organizes behaviour with reference to certain ends, it is an aspect of social organization as defined by Firth.[2]

The relationship of the labourers with management is characterized by both co-operation and conflict. The norms of the co-operative aspect of the relationship are regulated by individual wage contracts and the plantation administration. The main function of the ideology of *mati* is that it provides the basis for organizing the labourers in their conflict with management and (to a lesser degree) with institutions outside the plantation. The egalitarian ideology provides a means for ensuring solidarity and concerted action in the absence of any specific associations for this purpose. This generalization applies more to conditions before the recognition of trade unions by management (and the growth of political parties).[3] But, for a variety of reasons, the union has not proved to be an effective substitute. Further, confirming Simmel's contention that one party to a conflict is interested in seeing its opponent organized,[4] management has in recent times openly encouraged the union and this has had an adverse effect on the union's popularity with the labourers. The sudden and spontaneous strike is still the preferred form of expressing conflicting interests.

There is little faith in the Joint Committee. In addition to the reasons adduced in Chapter 4, I may mention here another anomaly of trade unionism and joint consultation in British Guiana. The meetings of the Joint Committee are as a rule presided over by the Administrative Manager. His drawing up of the agenda and conduct of the meeting, however impartial, does not prevent the labourers from feeling that justice does not seem to be done. There is widespread complaint that argument in the Joint Committee may be construed as insubordination and that little is to be gained from official arrangements for the resolution of differences. Again, election to the Joint Committee is held under management supervision, with a management official as the returning officer. There has been little to encourage the labourers to regard the union or the Joint Committee as organizations for prosecuting their interests effectively.

It is commonly believed that playing a leading role in trade disputes will eventually cause one to be marked as a trouble-maker and victimized. At present this is not a realistic belief and may well be a rationalization of a reluctance to assume leadership roles. Nevertheless the conviction is strong. In Blairmont the four labourer members of the Joint Committee who have

---

[1] Parsons, 1951, p. 350.   [2] Firth, 1955.
[3] The first political party was the People's Progressive Party formed in 1953 on the eve of the general election.   [4] Simmel, 1955, p. 90.

been most prominent in trade disputes for some time are all outsiders, i.e. urban or village residents.

In very recent times plantation labourers have been formally recognized as representatives of the union and fit and proper persons with whom negotiations can be conducted. Till then, salaried officials of the union had been brought in from outside. Management is also gradually beginning to accept the aggressive and vociferous opposition of labourer representatives who are compelled to impress their sceptical followers with their courage and devotion. If these trends continue and, in addition, there is less control of union decisions from the top, the position of the labourer representative will become more effective and he will not expect to be crushed between the opposing forces of management and labour which it is his duty to reconcile. This will reduce both unnecessary aggression and the inclination to feather one's own nest when conditions are still favourable. Public support of the union, in these circumstances, is bound to increase.

Of the present it can be said that the lack of any effective organization for the protection of its interests, lack of power to control matters of major importance, and lack of recognized bases of leadership give the egalitarian ideology a peculiar importance in the life of the plantation community.

A consideration of the social structure of the plantation shows that this ideology is not entirely unrealistic. Educational qualifications, income, property, and style of life mark the labourers as a distinct status group. This is emphasized still further by common residence, common subordination to management, and common subjection to the vagaries of the labour market. The changes in Indian culture may be partly interpreted as changes in the direction of intensifying recognition of the principle, 'Ah we all Indian.'

The official policies of the indenture period created a tradition of suffering and a conviction that coolies are an underprivileged group abandoned by those in power. The often repeated statement, 'Ah we coolie people proper punish', is one of those unifying mottoes about the destiny of its people found in many cultures. Amplified to 'Ah we coolie and black people proper punish' it serves as a basis for the solidarity of Negro and Indian rural dwellers. Actual and fictitious kinship links also intensify the awareness of being 'all de same'.

No person or institution in the community, with the exception of religious associations within a very limited sector, wields any real power. Authority to make far-reaching decisions affecting all aspects of the life of the group is vested in persons and institutions outside the community. All these features underline the homogeneous aspect of the social structure and constitute the 'empirical aspects of the interpretation of the nature and situation of the collectivity'.[1]

As Parsons states, every ideology has its non-empirical elements. The non-empirical element in the egalitarian ideology is its failure to take into

[1] Parsons, 1951, p. 350.

account what differentiation there is in the social system of the plantation. The organization of the labour force is individualistic: allocation of work and payment of wages are made to individuals and there are hardly any co-operative work groups. No individual has any effective control over the earning opportunities or wages of any other. A field labourer can find and hold a job in a gang regardless of his relations with the rest of the gang. Neither the gang, nor the union for that matter, can exercise any effective sanction against blacklegs. To my knowledge, no attempt has been made to boycott them.

Though the life-chances of labourers can, broadly speaking, be said to be the same, within these limits varying opportunities and capabilities result in locally significant differences and inequalities. As members of the wider society individual labourers are motivated towards achieving success, acquiring culturally valued goods and manners, and aiming at the upward mobility of their children. To this extent social reality does not correspond to the egalitarian ideology.

Certain institutions have the effect of maintaining the egalitarian ideology in the face of individual differentiation and divergences of interests and attitudes. One of these is drinking parties through which egalitarian sentiments are reiterated and reinforced. Heavy expenditure on rum also helps to siphon off wealth in excess of what is required to meet a basic standard of living. Production bonuses and strike pay increases are frequently spent on rum and luxuries. The lavishness of wedding feasts and the elaborate preparations at *pujas* and *kathas* are further instances of this. The accent on liberality levels economic inequalities and inhibits differentiation. The secularization of religious practices may be interpreted as providing further opportunities for the establishment of *mati*.

But these mechanisms cannot always reconcile the incompatibility between the egalitarian ideology and competition for prestige. *Eye-pass* disputes arise from this incompatibility. However, it is necessary, as Wright has pointed out,[1] to distinguish between incompatibility and conflict, for the former need not necessarily lead to the latter. The intervention of additional factors is necessary before a dispute is actually sparked.

To the extent that most plantation residents are affected by this incompatibility, it may be said that there is a potential tension between all residents which becomes an actual dispute when several other conditions are operative. Two such conditions were discussed in Chapter 5; that the contenders belong to the same status group, and that there should be regular interaction between them. This latter condition means, in effect, that *eye-pass* disputes tend to occur between persons living in the same neighbourhood.

These qualifications still include a large class of persons between whom *eye-pass* disputes can occur. However, an examination of the contenders in the disputes presented in Chapters 5–7 suggests a few other factors

[1] Wright, 1951.

which help to define this class more narrowly. It provides partial answers to the questions why some are more likely than others to make *eye-pass* accusations and why some rather than others are prone to be accused.

In the following analysis I include the private dispute underlying Example XIII and the two neighbours in Example V. I exclude Examples X and XI, which were not open disputes between identifiable opponents, and Example XII which was partly caused by the same dispute as that recorded in Example III. This provides a total of twenty-seven disputants. Although the disputes are typical, they have been selected rather for their illustrative value. The twenty-seven disputants are not a random sample and the conclusions I draw are therefore tentative.

One factor by which the disputants can be compared is age. The majority are between 31 and 50 years: two are under 31 and three are 50 and over; nine are between 41 and 50; thirteen are between 31 and 40. They are all married and household heads, except one of the disputants in Example VII who is unmarried and lives with his widowed mother; however, he is the virtual head of her household. Thus the disputants are for the most part socially mature adults in the period of greatest 'hustling' (to use the local term) in a man's life, when he seeks to acquire a respected position in the community for himself and his family both through his own efforts and the marriages and employment of his children. Another point to be noted is that the age differences between each set of contenders is not usually more than eight years. This figure is exceeded in Example IX (20 years), in the dispute between the clerk and the electrician who were brothers-in-law.

Of the twenty-seven disputants two are members of the Junior Staff, three are skilled labourers, and one is a goldsmith and 'dentist'. The rest are unskilled labourers. In the two disputes between persons belonging to different status groups (Examples I and IX) there are kinship ties between the disputants.

With the exception of Hassan in Example VIII the twenty unskilled labourers are relatively more successful than the average labourer and have claims to a greater prestige. For example, of the twenty labourers, eight held offices in one of the religious associations or in the Joint Committee, two owned cake-shops, one has been a clerk, one was the captain of a local cricket team and two were close relatives of drivers. One may relate these claims to greater prestige and the conflict they cause to the widespread association of poverty and humility with virtue. The following statement is an example, 'Me is a poor man and keep one-side; ah-we live good with all people and never get court story'. 'Keeping one-side' refers to the speaker's non-involvement in competition and conflict.

The conclusions that can be drawn from these considerations are that *eye-pass* disputes tend to occur between those persons who (*a*) are at the prestige-acquiring period of their lives, (*b*) are mature members of the community, (*c*) belong to the same age and status group and neighbourhood, (*d*) are relatively successful or claim to be so, (*d*) are held in some esteem or believe they are. Because they cannot be nailed down as typical 'punishing' coolies, relations between them can be bedevilled by some uncertainty as to exactly how they should behave towards one another. Their relations with one another present, to use Parsons' term, an 'unstructured situation' which raises problems of criteria for measuring the fulfilment of role-expectations.[1]

Eye-pass disputes need not necessarily be conducted violently, though most are. Whether a dispute is waged peacefully depends on the existence of some reciprocal relationship through which one contender can exercise sanctions against the other. Since there are few such relationships violence is the usual mode of conducting these disputes.

Disputes not caused by *eye-pass* seldom involve violence. In labour-management disputes sanctions are exercised through suspension from work, expulsion from the plantation, complaints to the Labour Inspector, and strikes. Disputes in religious associations are waged through theological controversy, formation of sects and factions, avoidance of church services, criticism and debate at public gatherings, and complaints to the manager. Quarrels about property, i.e. about objects borrowed and bought and about division of household effects on the decease of the head or on separation, are usually taken to the manager or, very occasionally, to the court. Marital disputes involve some cursing and wife-beating, but this sort of violence is not a public duel like an *eye-pass* dispute. None of these disputes, it may be noted, is a quarrel over the breach of egalitarian norms and therefore has no *eye-pass* connotations.

FUNCTIONS OF EYE-PASS DISPUTES

Eye-pass disputes may be described, in Simpson's terms, as 'communal conflict'. The dispute arises from a sharing of egalitarian values. An individual retaliates against a supposed slight because he believes himself to be entitled to prestige which is at least on a par with that of others. Conversely, his opponent pays heed to his counter-attack because it is publicly claimed that he is inferior to others. Even when an individual provokes a quarrel in order to demonstrate his superiority, his behaviour may be attributed to the lack of any standard of comparison and consequent insecurity. The attack is, as it were, a feint to test the other's ability to re-equalize prestige. *Eye-pass* disputes seldom result in any change in the structure of the group.

Indeed, the disputes may be described as an institution which helps to maintain the egalitarian social order. Coser points out that 'Conflict may serve to remove dissociating elements in a relationship, and to re-establish unity'. By claiming a superior prestige the *eye-pass* offender, in effect, withdraws from the egalitarian social group. But when he is attacked, his defence of counter-abuse and assault constitutes an appeal to the public

---

[1] Parsons, 1951, pp. 269–71.

which emphasizes a sense of community between the contenders and between them and their audience at the very moment when these bonds are called in question.

Both the assertion of superiority and its refutation are made through the same stylized idiom of abuse and assault, marking the quarrel as one between equals in power. Neither party gains a clear advantage and the resultant stalemate gives reality to the postulate that no-one is superior to another.

Eye-pass disputes may be described as regulated. The dispute is essentially a public event. The usual mode of attacking an opponent is such that it both presumes the existence of an audience and ensures its attendance. The sanctions against taking sides prevent the dispute from becoming a riot. The role of the public is to witness the claims and complaints and to stop the fight before any foolhardy act is committed. The contenders themselves, who join battle with cutlass and axe, have no intention of causing each other any serious injury. A dispute may be interpreted as a socially regulated safety-valve for the release of accumulated animosity between rivals. It also provides a temporary accommodation of conflicting interests.

Disputes elicit from the contenders' public avowal of egalitarian norms which are thus reaffirmed in spectacular fashion. Frequent spectacles educate the public in the norms, urge conformity to them, and impress on all the image of society as an association of equals. The violent quarrel also implicates the public and thereby stimulates mediatory processes.

In addition, the open quarrel is a means by which a dispute can be taken to the court. The violence is a method of converting an offence the court does not recognise into one which it will.

Eye-pass disputes are the expression of conflict between the egalitarian norms of the plantation community and the norms of individual achievement of the wider society. They are characterized by some of the conditions in which conflict assumes positive functions: they occur within a framework of accepted norms and values, their multiplicity inhibits unbridgeable cleavages, and their conduct is regulated up to a point.

The positive functions of *eye-pass* disputes refer to their contribution to the maintenance of the egalitarian social norms of the plantation and not to the maintenance of the total society. A mode of behaviour which is functional within the social system of a sub-group may well be dysfunctional in the wider society. *Eye-pass* disputes are produced by factors which especially affect the plantation and are functional relative to the importance of these factors in the social life of the group.

Further, as Bendix has suggested, 'it is probable that *every* social fact (minority status, crime, strikes, etc.) has some consequence *both* for the continued adaptation and for the impairment of the social structure'.[1] *Eye-pass* disputes, like several other expressions of conflict,[2] have both

---

[1] Bendix and Berger, 1959, p. 111.   [2] See the discussion of factions in Firth, 1957.

functions and dysfunctions. In this study I have been concerned mainly with the functions for, at present, the dysfunctions are less important. Yet these can become more pronounced in the rapidly changing society.

Change can affect both the status and the perspectives of plantation labourers as well as the composition of plantation communities. Whether the Guianese choose a Cuban or a Puerto Rican model, the position of plantation labourers is likely to change radically in the coming decade. With each general election labourers feel more confident of their ability to influence their destiny. The Extra-Nuclear Housing Schemes, the proposal to incorporate these settlements into the local government system, and the increasing importance of and access to political parties will restrict management-labour relations to the purely industrial sphere. The growth of unions more democratically controlled and with more labourer participation, the rise of a corps of management officials indoctrinated with the 'human relations' ideology of personnel management courses, better relations between Whites and other races, as well as the progressive Guianization of supervisory posts, all these trends will alter the nature of the class conflict which has been the background theme of this study.

Economic development will change the composition of plantation communities because new industries will provide opportunities for both occupational and economic mobility. Reclamation of land from the marshes and resettlement of surplus population from plantations were already under way in the Corentyne district during 1956–8. The company's mechanization plans, held up by a stagnant economy, envisage small residential communities of skilled technicians and reliance on villages for seasonal unskilled labour.

The more rapidly these changes (incipient in 1956–8) proceed, the more will the social patterns described here change, and the more will the dysfunctions of egalitarian norms and the consequent disputes be emphasized. They can act as an additional brake on upward social mobility and set a low ceiling for aspirations which will result in a failure to exploit fully all available opportunities. They inhibit the growth of effective leadership and consequently of voluntary, self-regulating associations through which many of the needs of a modern society are met. Leadership in associations such as local branches of political parties and trade unions passes by default to outsiders who could be unresponsive to local needs. By a process akin to Merton's 'self-fulfilling prophecy', the group's belief in its powerlessness continues to remain true.

Any analysis of social conflict should attempt to balance its functions against its dysfunctions. While disclaiming any pretence to accuracy in sociological book-keeping, I venture to suggest that *eye-pass* disputes help to maintain the egalitarian social norms which so far has provided the most effective assurance of the interests of the plantation labourers.

Appendix

TABLE I

Blairmont; Frequency of Cases—1949–56

Type of cases	1949	1950	1951	1952	1953	1954	1955	1956	Total	Per cent
Assault	24	15	11	15	17	20	20	39	161	12·6
Disorderly Behaviour	14	16	6	23	16	20	6	8	109	8·6
Provocative Language	20	25	20	30	40	36	33	35	239	18·8
Vagrancy and Drunkenness	1	0	2	3	1	1	1	1	10	0·8
Attempted Suicide	0	0	0	0	0	0	2	0	2	0·2
Larceny	13	12	1	8	2	6	3	7	52	4·1
Trespass (Criminal)	0	0	0	0	2	1	0	0	3	0·2
Injury to Property	2	2	0	0	1	0	0	0	5	0·4
Affiliation	5	10	6	11	4	6	16	14	72	5·7
Desertion and Maintenance	1	2	0	11	0	6	2	1	23	1·8
Education of Child	0	0	0	7	7	15	8	17	54	4·2
Traffic	6	10	5	11	9	3	6	15	65	5·1
Licences	3	4	5	3	0	1	2	35	53	4·2
Miscellaneous Offences	3	5	1	4	9	6	3	4	35	2·7
Damages	7	3	2	3	9	21	8	17	70	5·5
Detinue	5	2	4	1	6	6	0	3	27	2·1
Trespass (Civil)	0	0	0	0	0	0	0	0	0	0
Rent, Hire and Wages	9	2	4	9	8	6	5	7	50	3·9
Possession	1	1	2	2	0	0	5	4	15	1·2
Debt	17	18	13	32	40	27	26	46	219	17·2
Breach of Agreement	0	0	0	1	0	0	0	2	3	0·2
Judgment Costs	1	0	0	2	2	0	1	0	6	0·5
Total	132	127	82	176	173	181	147	255	1273	100·0

TABLE II

Bush Lot, West Coast Berbice; Frequency of Cases—1949–56

Type of cases	1949	1950	1951	1952	1953	1954	1955	1956	Total	Per cent
Assault	8	9	10	6	17	21	13	13	97	8·5
Disorderly Behaviour	4	6	2	7	6	9	3	10	47	4·1
Provocative Language	5	17	12	13	9	24	6	14	100	8·9
Vagrancy and Drunkenness	0	1	1	1	0	0	0	0	3	0·3
Attempted Suicide	0	0	0	0	0	0	0	0	0	0
Larceny	13	4	1	8	2	0	4	1	33	2·9
Trespass (Criminal)	1	3	6	0	0	6	0	4	20	1·8
Injury to Property	0	0	8	1	0	0	0	9	18	1·6
Affiliation	1	0	1	2	3	5	5	4	21	1·8
Desertion and Maintenance	1	5	2	0	0	0	5	2	15	1·3
Education of Child	0	0	0	0	0	0	0	9	9	0·8
Traffic	11	15	4	17	3	2	4	14	70	6·2
Licences	3	2	1	5	0	2	4	1	18	1·6
Miscellaneous Offences	7	21	4	8	5	8	6	4	62	5·4
Damages	24	21	16	25	25	29	20	29	189	16·6
Detinue	2	1	2	2	7	4	1	3	22	1·9
Trespass (Civil)	0	0	0	0	1	0	0	0	1	0·1
Rent, Hire and Wages	3	4	9	11	22	13	27	35	125	11·0
Possession	0	0	0	1	2	0	1	2	6	0·5
Debt	25	19	24	34	36	25	40	50	253	22·2
Breach of Agreement	1	0	1	2	1	0	1	7	13	1·1
Judgment Costs	3	2	1	0	1	2	1	6	16	1·4
Total	112	130	105	143	140	150	141	217	1138	100·0

TABLE III

Port Mourant; Frequency of Cases—1953–7

Type of cases	1953	1954	1955	1956	1957	Total	Per cent
Assault	61	103	117	80	115	476	17·9
Disorderly Behaviour	33	52	41	34	57	217	8·2
Provocative Language	41	124	126	63	116	470	17·7
Vagrancy and Drunkenness	1	1	4	1	4	11	0·4
Attempted Suicide	5	0	0	0	1	6	0·2
Larceny	4	22	12	18	17	73	2·8
Trespass (Criminal)	0	1	9	3	5	18	0·7
Injury to Property	2	2	4	3	7	18	0·7
Affiliation	5	17	18	3	19	62	2·3
Desertion and Maintenance	5	34	61	47	56	203	7·7
Education of Child	0	0	0	0	0	0	0
Traffic	7	15	30	37	21	110	4·1
Licences	3	13	17	5	6	44	1·7
Miscellaneous Offences	20	44	43	37	22	166	6·3
Damages	64	40	44	49	21	218	8·2
Detinue	1	4	8	3	3	19	0·7
Trespass (Civil)	0	0	1	0	0	1	0
Rent, Hire and Wages	11	11	24	25	10	81	3·1
Possession	9	6	5	3	2	25	0·9
Debt	77	78	84	100	66	405	15·3
Breach of Agreement	2	3	2	0	0	7	0·3
Judgment Costs	2	10	3	5	2	22	0·8
Total	353	580	653	516	550	2652	100·0

TABLE IV

Bush Lot, Corentyne; Frequency of Cases—1953-7

Type of cases	1953	1954	1955	1956	1957	Total	Per cent
Assault	6	2	5	5	4	22	5·3
Disorderly Behaviour	1	3	6	7	5	22	5·3
Provocative Language	9	8	6	4	11	38	9·1
Vagrancy and Drunkenness	0	0	0	0	0	0	0
Attempted Suicide	0	0	0	0	0	0	0
Larceny	3	3	0	2	1	9	2·2
Trespass (Criminal)	0	2	2	0	0	4	1·0
Injury to Property	1	4	0	0	1	6	1·4
Affiliation	0	0	0	0	0	0	0
Desertion and Maintenance	3	0	4	5	1	13	3·1
Education of Child	0	0	5	0	0	5	1·2
Traffic	6	5	5	4	7	27	6·5
Licences	0	3	0	1	0	4	1·0
Miscellaneous Offences	2	1	2	3	9	17	4·1
Damages	19	19	26	10	25	99	23·9
Detinue	2	1	2	1	1	7	1·7
Trespass (Civil)	0	0	0	0	2	2	0·5
Rent, Hire and Wages	5	6	7	14	12	44	10·6
Possession	3	0	0	3	1	7	1·7
Debt	9	13	17	17	21	77	18·5
Breach of Agreement	2	1	0	2	0	5	1·2
Judgment Costs	0	1	3	2	1	7	1·7
Total	71	72	90	80	102	415	100·0

TABLE V

Port Mourant; Criminal Cases Classified by Action and Result—1953-7

Type of cases	Order made	Fined	Jailed	Committed	Repri- manded and dis- charged	Dis- mis- sed	With- drawn	N.A.P.S.O.*	Total
Assault	0	180	11	1	33	47	103	101	476
Disorderly Behaviour	0	128	3	0	31	11	26	18	217
Provocative Language	0	82	0	0	14	48	132	194	470
Vagrancy and Drunkenness	0	7	0	0	0	2	2	0	11
Attempted Suicide	0	0	0	0	6	0	0	0	6
Larceny	0	27	3	3	7	14	16	3	73
Trespass	0	5	0	0	2	0	5	6	18
Injury to Property	0	9	0	0	4	2	3	0	18
Affiliation	35	8	1	1	0	3	3	11	62
Desertion and Maintenance	51	9	0	0	0	1	42	100	203
Education of Child	0	0	0	0	0	0	0	0	0
Traffic	0	79	0	0	16	2	10	3	110
Licences	0	22	4	0	10	1	7	0	44
Miscellaneous Offences	5	76	2	3	32	5	30	13	166
Total	91	632	24	8	155	136	379	449	1,874

* 'No appearance of parties—struck out.'

TABLE VI

Bush Lot, Corentyne; Criminal Cases Classified by Action and Result—1953–7

Type of cases	Order made	Fined	Jailed	Committed	Reprimanded and discharged	Dismissed	Withdrawn	N.A.P.S.O.*	Total
Assault	0	10	0	0	2	4	2	4	22
Disorderly Behaviour	0	14	0	0	4	3	0	1	22
Provocative Language	0	13	0	0	2	1	3	19	38
Vagrancy and Drunkenness	0	0	0	0	0	0	0	0	0
Attempted Suicide	0	0	0	0	0	0	0	0	0
Larceny	0	3	2	0	2	2	0	0	9
Trespass	0	0	0	0	0	1	1	2	4
Injury to Property	0	1	0	0	0	2	2	1	6
Affiliation	0	0	0	0	0	0	0	0	0
Desertion and Maintenance	4	1	0	0	0	0	2	6	13
Education of Child	1	0	0	0	0	0	4	0	5
Traffic	0	19	0	0	4	1	3	0	27
Licences	0	3	0	0	0	0	1	0	4
Miscellaneous Offences	0	9	0	0	3	0	2	3	17
Total	5	73	2	0	17	14	20	36	167

* 'No appearance of parties—struck out.'

TABLE VII

Port Mourant; Civil Cases Classified by Action and Result—1953–7

Type of cases	Judg-ment awarded	Judg-ment by consent	Dis-missed	Set-tled	With-drawn	N.A.P.S.O.*	Total
Damages	35	31	6	36	42	68	218
Detinue	5	2	0	0	5	7	19
Trespass	0	0	0	0	0	1	1
Rent, Hire and Wages	15	15	4	7	15	25	81
Possession	5	2	0	0	11	7	25
Debt	137	102	4	31	33	98	405
Breach of Agreement	5	0	0	0	1	1	7
Judgment Costs	10	2	0	0	3	7	22
Total	212	154	14	74	110	214	778

* 'No appearance of parties—struck out.'

TABLE VIII

Bush Lot, Corentyne; Civil Cases Classified by Action and Result—1953–7

Type of cases	Judg-ment awarded	Judg-ment by consent	Dis-missed	Set-tled	With-drawn	N.A.P.S.O.*	Total
Damages	19	11	4	22	13	30	99
Detinue	3	0	1	0	1	2	7
Trespass	0	0	0	0	1	1	2
Rent, Hire and Wages	7	11	0	10	8	8	44
Possession	2	1	0	2	2	0	7
Debt	22	15	0	15	8	17	77
Breach of Agreement	1	1	0	0	1	2	5
Judgment Costs	1	3	0	0	1	2	7
Total	55	42	5	49	35	62	248

* 'No appearance of parties—struck out.'

References

ADAMS, R. N., 1959. 'On the Relation between Plantation and Creole Cultures', in *Plantation Systems of the New World*. Pan American Union, Washington.

AMOS, S., 1871. *The Existing Laws of Demerara for the Regulation of Coolie Emigration*, London.

BACON, SELDEN B., 1958. 'Alcoholics do not drink', in *Understanding Alcoholism, Annals of the American Academy of Political and Social Science*, Vol. 315, Philadelphia.

BEAUMONT, J., 1871. *The New Slavery*. London.

BENDIX, R., and BERGER, B., 1959. 'Images of Society and Problems of Concept Formation in Sociology', in ed. L. Gross, *Symposium on Sociological Theory*. New York.

BERNARD, J., 1957a. 'Parties and Issues in Conflict', *Conflict Resolution*, Vol. 1, No. 2.

— 1957b. 'The Sociological Study of Conflict', in *The Nature of Conflict*. International Sociological Association, Unesco, Paris.

BRAITHWAITE, L., 1953. 'Social Stratification in Trinidad', *Social and Economic Studies*, Vol. 2, Nos. 2 and 3.

BRONKHURST, H. V. P., 1883. *British Guiana and its Labouring Population*. London.

COMINS, D. W. D., 1893. *Notes on Emigration from India to British Guiana*. Calcutta.

COSER, L., 1956. *The Functions of Social Conflict*. Glencoe, Illinois.

— 1957. 'Social Conflict and Social Change', *British Journal of Sociology*, Vol. 7, No. 3.

DAHRENDORF, R., 1958a. 'Towards a Theory of Social Conflict', *Conflict Resolution*, Vol. 2, No. 2.

— 1958b. 'Out of Utopia: Towards a Re-Orientation of Sociological Analysis', *American Journal of Sociology*, Vol. 64, No. 2.

— 1959. *Class and Class Conflict in Industrial Society*. London.

DALTON, H. G., 1855. *The History of British Guiana* (2 vols.). London.

DENNIS, N., HENRIQUES, F., and SLAUGHTER, C., 1956. *Coal is Our Life*. London.

DES VOEUX, SIR G. W., 1948. *Experiences of a Demerara Magistrate*. Georgetown. (Reprint of Chapters 1–9 of Des Voeux, *My Colonial Service*, 2 vols., London, 1903.)

DUBE, S. C., 1954. *Indian Village*. London.

EPSTEIN, A. L., 1958. *Politics in an Urban African Community*. Manchester.

EVANS-PRITCHARD, E. E., 1937. *Witchcraft, Oracles and Magic among the Azande*. Oxford.

FIRTH, R. W., 1951. *Elements of Social Organisation*. London.

— 1954. 'Social Organisation and Social Change', *Journal of the Royal Anthropological Institute*, Vol. 84.

— 1955. 'Some Principles of Social Organisation', *Journal of the Royal Anthropological Institute*, Vol. 85.

— 1957. 'Introduction' to 'Factions in Indian and Overseas Societies', *British Journal of Sociology*, Vol. 8, No. 4.

FORTES, M., 1940. 'Political System of the Tallensi', in ed. Fortes and Evand-Pritchard, *African Political Systems*. London.

— 1953. 'The Structure of Unilineal Descent Groups.' *American Anthropologist*, Vol. 55.

FRANKENBERG, R., 1957. *Village on the Border*. London.

GARDNER, B., 1946. 'The Factory as a Social System', in ed. W. F. Whyte, *Industry and Society*. New York.

GLUCKMAN, M., 1940. 'Analysis of a Social Situation in Modern Zululand', *Bantu Studies*, Vol. 14.

— 1954a. 'Political Institutions', in Evans-Pritchard *et al.*, *Institutions of Primitive Society*. Oxford.

— 1954b. *Rituals of Rebellion in South-East Africa*. Manchester.

— 1955a. *Judicial Process among the Barotse*. Manchester.

— 1955b. *Custom and Conflict in Africa*. Oxford.

HARRIS, J. H., c. 1910. *Coolie Labour in the British Crown Colonies and Protectorates*. London.

HERSKOVITS, M. J. and F. S., 1936. *Suriname Folklore*. New York.

JAGAN, C., c. 1953. *Bitter Sugar*. Georgetown.

— 1954. *Forbidden Freedom*. London.

JAYAWARDENA, C., 1960. 'Marital Stability in Two Guianese Sugar Estate Communities', *Social and Economic Studies*, Vol. 9, No. 1.

— 1962. 'Family Organisation in Plantations in British Guiana', *International Journal of Comparative Sociology*, Vol. 3, No. 1.

JENKINS, E., 1871. *The Coolie, His Rights and Wrongs*. London.

KELLER, MARK, 1958. 'Alcoholism: Nature and Extent of the Problem', in *Understanding Alcoholism, Annals of the American Academy of Political and Social Science*, Vol. 315, Philadelphia.

LEACH, E. R., 1954. *Political Systems of Highland Burma*. London.

LEWIS, A. W., 1939. *Labour in the West Indies*. London.

MARRIOTT, M., 1955. *Village India*. Chicago.

MERTON, R. K., 1958. *Social Theory and Social Structure*. Revised edition. Glencoe, Illinois.

MINTZ, S. W., and WOLF, E. R., 1957. 'Haciendas and Plantations in Middle America and the Antilles', *Social and Economic Studies*, Vol. 6, No. 3.

NADEL, S. F., 1952. 'Witchcraft in Four African Societies', *American Anthropologist*, Vol. 54, No. 1.

NATH, D., 1950. *History of the Indians in British Guiana*. London.

Overseer's Manual (2nd ed.), Georgetown, 1887.

PARSONS, T., 1951. *The Social System*. Glencoe, Illinois.

— 1954. *Essays in Sociological Theory*. Glencoe, Illinois.

RADCLIFFE-BROWN, A. R., 1952. *Structure and Function in Primitive Society*. London.

Reports

1872. *Coolie Riots in Essequibo : a Report of the Proceedings and Evidence at the Inquest of the Bodies of Five Rioters Killed by the Fire of the Police.* Georgetown.

1924. *The Ruimveldt Inquiry : Coroner's Report.* Georgetown.

1949. *Report of a Commission of Inquiry into the Sugar Industry of British Guiana.* H.M.S.O., London.

1956. *Annual Report of the Registrar-General for the Year 1952.* Georgetown.

1957. *Report on British Guiana.* H.M.S.O., London.

RODWAY, J., 1891–4. *History of British Guiana* (3 vols.). Georgetown.

RUHOMON, P., 1939. *Centenary History of the East Indians in British Guiana, 1838–1938.* Georgetown.

SCHUMPETER, J., 1955. *Social Classes and Imperialism,* trans. by H. Norden. Meridian Books, New York.

SIMMEL, G., 1955. *Conflict and The Web of Group Affiliations,* trans. by K. Wolf and R. Bendix. Glencoe, Illinois.

SIMPSON, G., 1937, *Community and Conflict.* New York.

SINGH, K. M., 1925. *Report on a Deputation to British Guiana.* Calcutta.

SKINNER, E. P., 1955. *Ethnic Interaction in a British Guiana Rural Community.* (Unpublished Ph.D. Thesis, Columbia University.)

— 1960. 'Group Dynamics and Social Stratification in British Guiana', in ed. Rubin, V., *Social and Cultural Pluralism in the Caribbean (Annals of the New York Academy of Sciences,* Vol. 83). New York.

SMITH, M. G., 1955. *A Framework for Caribbean Studies.* U.C.W.I., Jamaica.

SMITH, R. T., 1956. *The Negro Family in British Guiana.* London.

— 1957a. *A Preliminary Report on a Rice-Growing Community in British Guiana* (unpublished).

— 1957b. 'Rice Production in an East Indian Community in British Guiana', *Social and Economic Studies,* Vol. 6, No. 4.

— 1959. 'Some Social Characteristics of Indian Immigrants to British Guiana', *Population Studies,* Vol. 13, No. 1.

SMITH, R. T., and JAYAWARDENA, C., 1958. 'Hindu Marriage Customs in British Guiana', *Social and Economic Studies,* Vol. 7, No. 2.

— 1959. 'Family and Marriage amongst East Indians in British Guiana', *Social and Economic Studies,* Vol. 8, No. 4.

STEVENSON, H. N. C., 1954. 'Status Evaluation in the Hindu Caste System', *Journal of the Royal Anthropological Institute,* Vol. 84.

TROLLOPE, A., 1867. *The West Indies and the Spanish Main.* London.

TURNER, V. W., 1957. *Schism and Continuity in an African Society.* Manchester.

TYSON, J. D., 1939. *Report on the Condition of Indians in Jamaica, British Guiana and Trinidad.* Simla.

WAGLEY, C., 1957. 'Plantation America, a Cultural Sphere', in ed. Rubin, V., *Caribbean Studies.* Jamaica.

WARNER, L., 1931. 'Murngin Warfare', *Oceania,* Vol. 1, No. 4.

WARNER, L., MEEKER, M., and EELS, K., 1949. *Social Class in America.* Chicago.

WEBER, M., 1947. *Theory of Social and Economic Organisation*, trans. by Henderson and Parsons. Glencoe, Illinois.

— 1958. *From Max Weber: Essays in Sociology*, trans. by Gerth and Mills. New York.

WEDGWOOD, C., 1930a. 'Some Aspects of Warfare in Melanesia', *Oceania*, Vol. 1, No. 1.

— 1930b. 'The Nature and Functions of Secret Societies', *Oceania*, Vol. 1, No. 2.

WHITFIELD, R. H., 1872. *The Present Position and Future Prospects of British Guiana, Second Letter*. London.

WRIGHT, Q., 1951. 'The Nature of Conflict', *The Western Political Quarterly*, Vol. 4, No. 2.

Index

For Product Safety Concerns and Information please contact our EU
representative GPSR@taylorandfrancis.com
Taylor & Francis Verlag GmbH, Kaufingerstraße 24, 80331 München, Germany

www.ingramcontent.com/pod-product-compliance
Ingram Content Group UK Ltd.
Pitfield, Milton Keynes, MK11 3LW, UK
UKHW020948180425
457613UK00019B/586